CRYPTOGRAPHY, STEGANOGRAPHY AND DATA SECURITY

U.S. NATIONAL CYBERSECURITY

STRATEGIC CHALLENGES AND OPPORTUNITIES

Cryptography, Steganography and Data Security

Additional books in this series can be found on Nova's website under the Series tab.

Additional e-books in this series can be found on Nova's website under the e-book tab.

CRYPTOGRAPHY, STEGANOGRAPHY AND DATA SECURITY

U.S. NATIONAL CYBERSECURITY

STRATEGIC CHALLENGES AND OPPORTUNITIES

GRACE POWERS
EDITOR

nova publishers
New York

Additional color graphics may be available in the e-book version of this book.

Library of Congress Cataloging-in-Publication Data

ISBN: 978-1-63321-831-4

Published by Nova Science Publishers, Inc. † New York

CONTENTS

PREFACE

This book identifies challenges faced by the federal government in addressing a strategic approach to cybersecurity, and determines the extent to which the national cybersecurity strategy adheres to desirable characteristics for such a strategy.

Chapter 1 – Cyber attacks could have a potentially devastating impact on the nation's computer systems and networks, disrupting the operations of government and businesses and the lives of private individuals. Increasingly sophisticated cyber threats have underscored the need to manage and bolster the cybersecurity of key government systems as well as the nation's critical infrastructure. GAO has designated federal information security as a government-wide high-risk area since 1997, and in 2003 expanded it to include cyber critical infrastructure. GAO has issued numerous reports since that time making recommendations to address weaknesses in federal information security programs as well as efforts to improve critical infrastructure protection. Over that same period, the executive branch has issued strategy documents that have outlined a variety of approaches for dealing with persistent cybersecurity issues.

GAO's objectives were to (1) identify challenges faced by the federal government in addressing a strategic approach to cybersecurity, and (2) determine the extent to which the national cybersecurity strategy adheres to desirable characteristics for such a strategy. To address these objectives, GAO analyzed previous reports and updated information obtained from officials at federal agencies with key cybersecurity responsibilities. GAO also obtained the views of experts in information technology management and cybersecurity and conducted a survey of chief information officers at major federal agencies.

Chapter 2 – Report of President's Council of Advisors on Science and Technology on Immediate Opportunities for Strengthening the Nation's Cybersecurity.

In: U.S. National Cybersecurity
Editor: Grace Powers
ISBN: 978-1-63321-831-4

Chapter 1

CYBERSECURITY: NATIONAL STRATEGY, ROLES, AND RESPONSIBILITIES NEED TO BE BETTER DEFINED AND MORE EFFECTIVELY IMPLEMENTED*

United States Government Accountability Office

WHY GAO DID THIS STUDY

Cyber attacks could have a potentially devastating impact on the nation's computer systems and networks, disrupting the operations of government and businesses and the lives of private individuals. Increasingly sophisticated cyber threats have underscored the need to manage and bolster the cybersecurity of key government systems as well as the nation's critical infrastructure. GAO has designated federal information security as a government-wide high-risk area since 1997, and in 2003 expanded it to include cyber critical infrastructure. GAO has issued numerous reports since that time making recommendations to address weaknesses in federal information security programs as well as efforts to improve critical infrastructure protection. Over that same period, the executive branch has issued strategy documents that have outlined a variety of approaches for dealing with persistent cybersecurity issues.

---

* This is an edited, reformatted and augmented version of the United States Government Accountability Office publication, GAO-13-187, dated February 2013.

GAO's objectives were to (1) identify challenges faced by the federal government in addressing a strategic approach to cybersecurity, and (2) determine the extent to which the national cybersecurity strategy adheres to desirable characteristics for such a strategy. To address these objectives, GAO analyzed previous reports and updated information obtained from officials at federal agencies with key cybersecurity responsibilities. GAO also obtained the views of experts in information technology management and cybersecurity and conducted a survey of chief information officers at major federal agencies.

GAO and inspector general reports have identified a number of key challenge areas in the federal government's approach to cybersecurity, including those related to protecting the nation's critical infrastructure. While actions have been taken to address aspects of these, issues remain in each of these challenge areas, including:

- **Designing and implementing risk-based federal and critical infrastructure programs.** Shortcomings persist in assessing risks, developing and implementing controls, and monitoring results in both the federal government and critical infrastructure. For example, in the federal arena, 8 of 22 major agencies reported compliance with risk management requirements under the Federal Information Security Management Act (FISMA), down from 13 out of 24 the year before. In the critical infrastructure arena, the Department of Homeland Security (DHS) and the other sector- specific agencies have not yet identified cybersecurity guidance applicable to or widely used in each of the critical sectors. GAO has continued to make numerous recommendations to address weaknesses in risk management processes at individual federal agencies and to further efforts by sector-specific agencies to enhance critical infrastructure protection.
- **Detecting, responding to, and mitigating cyber incidents**. DHS has made incremental progress in coordinating the federal response to cyber incidents, but challenges remain in sharing information among federal agencies and key private sector entities, including critical infrastructure owners, as well as in developing a timely analysis and warning capability. Difficulties in sharing and accessing classified information and the lack of a centralized information-sharing system continue to hinder progress. According to DHS, a secure environment for sharing cybersecurity information, at all classification levels, is not expected to be fully operational until fiscal year 2018. Further, although DHS has taken steps to establish timely analysis and

warning, GAO previously reported that the department had yet to establish a predictive analysis capability and recommended that DHS expand capabilities to investigate incidents. According to the department, tools for predictive analysis are to be tested in fiscal year 2013.

- **Promoting education, awareness, and workforce planning**. In November 2011, GAO reported that agencies leading strategic planning efforts for education and awareness, including Commerce, the Office of Management and Budget (OMB), the Office of Personnel Management, and DHS, had not developed details on how they were going to achieve planned outcomes and that the specific tasks and responsibilities were unclear. GAO recommended, among other things, that the key federal agencies involved in the initiative collaborate to clarify responsibilities and processes for planning and monitoring their activities. GAO also reported that only 2 of 8 agencies it reviewed developed cyber workforce plans and only 3 of the 8 agencies had a department-wide training program for their cybersecurity workforce. GAO recommended that these agencies take a number of steps to improve agency and government-wide cybersecurity workforce efforts. The agencies generally agreed with the recommendations.
- **Promoting research and development (R&D)**. The goal of supporting targeted cyber R&D has been impeded by implementation challenges among federal agencies. In June 2010, GAO reported that R&D initiatives were hindered by limited sharing of detailed information about ongoing research, including the lack of a repository to track R&D projects and funding, as required by law. GAO recommended that a mechanism be established for tracking ongoing and completed federal cybersecurity R&D projects and associated funding, and that this mechanism be utilized to develop an ongoing process to make federal R&D information available to federal agencies and the private sector. However, as of September 2012, this mechanism had not yet been fully developed.
- **Addressing international cybersecurity challenges**. While progress has been made in identifying the importance of international cooperation and assigning roles and responsibilities related to it, the government's approach to addressing international aspects of cybersecurity has not yet been completely defined and implemented. GAO recommended in July 2010 that the government develop an

international strategy that specified outcome-oriented performance metrics and timeframes for completing activities. While an international strategy for cyberspace has been developed, it does not fully specify outcome-oriented performance metrics or timeframes for completing activities.

The government has issued a variety of strategy-related documents over the last decade, many of which address aspects of the above challenge areas. The documents address priorities for enhancing cybersecurity within the federal government as well as for encouraging improvements in the cybersecurity of critical infrastructure within the private sector. However, no overarching cybersecurity strategy has been developed that articulates priority actions, assigns responsibilities for performing them, and sets timeframes for their completion. In 2004, GAO developed a set of desirable characteristics that can enhance the usefulness of national strategies in allocating resources, defining policies, and helping to ensure accountability. Existing cybersecurity strategy documents have included selected elements of these desirable characteristics, such as setting goals and subordinate objectives, but have generally lacked other key elements. The missing elements include:

- **Milestones and performance measures**. The government's strategy documents include few milestones or performance measures, making it difficult to track progress in accomplishing stated goals and objectives. The lack of milestones and performance measures at the strategic level is mirrored in similar shortcomings within key government programs that are part of the government-wide strategy. The DHS inspector general, for example, recommended in 2011 that DHS develop and implement performance measures to be used to track and evaluate the effectiveness of actions defined in its strategic implementation plan. As of January 2012, DHS had not yet developed the performance measures but planned to do so.
- **Cost and resources**. While past strategy documents linked certain activities to budget submissions, none have fully addressed cost and resources, including justifying the required investment, which is critical to gaining support for implementation. In addition, none provided full assessments of anticipated costs and how resources might be allocated to address them.
- **Roles and responsibilities**. Cybersecurity strategy documents have assigned high-level roles and responsibilities but have left important

details unclear. Several GAO reports have likewise demonstrated that the roles and responsibilities of key agencies charged with protecting the nation's cyber assets are inadequately defined. For example, the chartering directives for several offices within the Department of Defense assign overlapping roles and responsibilities for preparing for and responding to domestic cyber incidents. In an October 2012 report, GAO recommended that the department update its guidance on preparing for and responding to domestic cyber incidents to include a description of its roles and responsibilities. In addition, it is unclear how OMB and DHS are to share oversight of individual departments and agencies. While the law gives OMB responsibility for oversight of federal government information security, OMB transferred several of its oversight responsibilities to DHS. Both DHS and OMB have issued annual FISMA reporting instructions to agencies, which could create confusion among agency officials because the instructions vary in content. Clarifying oversight responsibilities is a topic that could be effectively addressed through legislation.

- **Linkage with other key strategy documents**. Existing cybersecurity strategy documents vary in terms of priorities and structure, and do not specify how they link to or supersede other documents, nor do they describe how they fit into an overarching national cybersecurity strategy. For example, in 2012, the administration determined that trusted Internet connections, continuous monitoring, and strong authentication should be cross-agency priorities, but no explanation was given as to how these three relate to priorities previously established in other strategy documents.

The many continuing cybersecurity challenges faced by the government highlight the need for a clearly defined oversight process to ensure agencies are held accountable for implementing effective information security programs. Further, until an overarching national cybersecurity strategy is developed that addresses all key elements of desirable characteristics, overall progress in achieving the government's objectives is likely to remain limited.

What GAO Recommends

To address missing elements in the national cybersecurity strategy, such as milestones and performance measures, cost and resources, roles and responsibilities, and linkage with other key strategy documents, GAO recommends that the White House Cybersecurity Coordinator develop an overarching federal cybersecurity strategy that includes all key elements of the desirable characteristics of a national strategy. Such a strategy would provide a more effective framework for implementing cybersecurity activities and better ensure that such activities will lead to progress in cybersecurity.

This strategy should also better ensure that federal departments and agencies are held accountable for making significant improvements in cybersecurity challenge areas, including designing and implementing risk-based programs; detecting, responding to, and mitigating cyber incidents; promoting education, awareness, and workforce planning; promoting R&D; and addressing international cybersecurity challenges. To address these issues, the strategy should (1) clarify how OMB will oversee agency implementation of requirements for effective risk management processes and (2) establish a roadmap for making significant improvements in cybersecurity challenge areas where previous recommendations have not been fully addressed.

Further, to address ambiguities in roles and responsibilities that have resulted from recent executive branch actions, GAO believes Congress should consider legislation to better define roles and responsibilities for implementing and overseeing federal information security programs and for protecting the nation's critical cyber assets.

In its comments, the Executive Office of the President agreed that more needs to be done to develop a coherent and comprehensive strategy on cybersecurity but did not believe producing another strategy document would be beneficial. However, GAO believes an overarching strategy document that includes milestones and performance measures, cost and resources, roles and responsibilities, and linkage with other key strategy documents would provide a more effective framework for implementing cybersecurity activities. The Executive Office of the President also agreed that Congress should consider enhanced cybersecurity legislation.

What GAO Found

Threats to systems supporting critical infrastructure and federal operations are evolving and growing. Federal agencies have reported increasing numbers of cybersecurity incidents that have placed sensitive information at risk, with potentially serious impacts on federal and military operations; critical infrastructure; and the confidentiality, integrity, and availability of sensitive government, private sector, and personal information. The increasing risks are demonstrated by the dramatic increase in reports of security incidents, the ease of obtaining and using hacking tools, and steady advances in the sophistication and effectiveness of attack technology. As shown in the figure below, the number of incidents reported by federal agencies to the U.S. Computer Emergency Readiness Team has increased 782 percent from 2006 to 2012.

ABBREVIATIONS

CIO	chief information officer
CNCI	Comprehensive National Cybersecurity Initiative
CS&C	Office of Cybersecurity and Communication
DHS	Department of Homeland Security
DOD	Department of Defense
DOT	Department of Transportation
E^3A	EINSTEIN 3 Accelerated
FISMA	Federal Information Security Management Act
GPRA	Government Performance and Results Act
HHS	Department of Health and Human Services
HSPD-7	Homeland Security Presidential Directive 7
ISAC	Information Sharing and Analysis Center
JACKE	Joint Agency Cyber Knowledge Exchange
NASA	National Aeronautics and Space Administration
NCCIC	National Cybersecurity and Communications Integration Center
NICE	National Initiative for Cybersecurity Education
NIPP	National Infrastructure Protection Plan
NIST	National Institute of Standards and Technology
NITRD	Subcommittee on Networking and Information Technology Research and Development
OMB	Office of Management and Budget
OPM	Office of Personnel Management
OSTP	Office of Science and Technology Policy
R&D	research and development
TSP	Thrift Savings Plan
US-CERT	United States Computer Emergency Readiness Team
USGCB	United States Government Configuration Baseline
VA	Department of Veterans Affairs

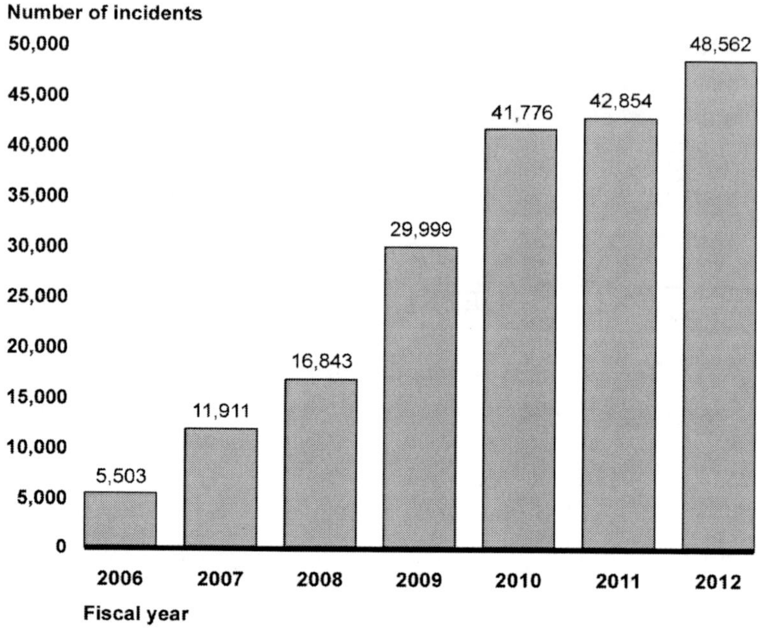

Source: GAO analysis of US-CERT data for fiscal years 2006-2012.

Incidents Reported by Federal Agencies in Fiscal Years 2006-2012.

***

February 14, 2013

Congressional Addressees

The pervasive use of the Internet has revolutionized the way that our government, our nation, and the rest of the world communicates and conducts business. While the benefits have been enormous, this widespread connectivity also poses significant risks to the government's and our nation's computer systems and networks as well as the critical operations and key infrastructures they support. The speed and accessibility that create the enormous benefits of the computer age, if not properly controlled, can allow unauthorized individuals and organizations to inexpensively eavesdrop on or interfere with these operations from remote locations for potentially malicious purposes, including fraud or sabotage. Increasingly sophisticated cyber threats have underscored the need to manage and bolster the cybersecurity of key government systems as well as the nation's critical infrastructure.[1]

Federal law and policy call for a risk-based approach to managing cybersecurity within the government and also specify activities to enhance the cybersecurity of public and private infrastructures that are essential to national security, national economic security, and public health and safety.[2] Over the last 12 years, the federal government has developed a number of strategies and plans for addressing cybersecurity based on this legal framework, including the National Strategy to Secure Cyberspace, issued in February 2003, and subsequent plans and strategies that address specific sectors, issues, and revised priorities.

We performed our work on the initiative of the U.S. Comptroller General to evaluate the federal government's cybersecurity strategies and understand the status of federal cybersecurity efforts to address challenges in establishing a strategic cybersecurity approach. Our objectives were to (1) determine the extent to which the national cybersecurity strategy includes key desirable characteristics of effective strategies, and (2) identify challenges faced by the federal government in addressing a strategic approach to cybersecurity.

To address our objectives, we analyzed key documents that reflect the federal government's evolving cybersecurity strategy, as well as other pertinent national strategies to determine the extent to which they included GAO's key desirable characteristics of a national strategy. In addition, we reviewed our previous reports and reports by agency inspectors general to identify key challenge areas. We also interviewed representatives from federal agencies with government-wide responsibilities for cybersecurity, including the Executive Office of the President, Office of Management and Budget (OMB), the Departments of Homeland Security (DHS) and Defense (DOD), and the National Institute of Standards and Technology (NIST), to obtain their views on cybersecurity issues as well as updated information about strategic initiatives. We also obtained expert perspective on key issues through use of two expert panels as well as surveys of cybersecurity experts and the chief information officers (CIO) of the 24 major federal agencies covered by the Chief Financial Officers Act.[3]

We conducted this performance audit from April 2012 to February 2013 in accordance with generally accepted government auditing standards. Those standards require that we plan and perform the audit to obtain sufficient, appropriate evidence to provide a reasonable basis for our findings and conclusions based on our audit objectives. We believe that the evidence obtained provides a reasonable basis for our findings and conclusions based on our audit objectives. A full description of our objectives, scope, and methodology can be found in appendix I. In addition, the names of cybersecurity and information management experts participating in our two expert panels, as well as participants in our expert survey and CIO survey, can be found in appendix II.

BACKGROUND

Threats to systems supporting critical infrastructure and federal information systems are evolving and growing. Advanced persistent threats—where adversaries that possess sophisticated levels of expertise and significant resources to pursue its objectives repeatedly over an extended period of time—pose increasing risks. In 2009, the President declared the cyber threat to be "[o]ne of the most serious economic and national security challenges we face as a nation" and stated that "America's economic prosperity in the 21st century will depend on cybersecurity."[4] The Director of National Intelligence has also warned of the increasing globalization of cyber attacks, including those carried out by foreign militaries or organized international crime. In January 2012, he testified that such threats pose a critical national and economic security concern.[5] To further highlight the importance of the threat, on October 11, 2012, the Secretary of Defense stated that the collective result of attacks on our nation's critical infrastructure could be "a cyber Pearl Harbor; an attack that would cause physical destruction and the loss of life."[6] These growing and evolving threats can potentially affect all segments of our society, including individuals, private businesses, government agencies, and other entities. We have identified the protection of federal information systems as a high-risk area for the government since 1997.[7] In 2003, this high-risk area was expanded to include protecting systems supporting our nation's critical infrastructure. Each year since that time, GAO has issued multiple reports detailing weaknesses in federal information security programs and making recommendations to address them. A list of key GAO products can be found at the end of this report.

Sources of Threats and Attack Methods Vary

The evolving array of cyber-based threats facing the nation pose threats to national security, commerce and intellectual property, and individuals.

Table 1. Sources of Adversarial Threats to Cybersecurity

Threat source	Description
Bot-network operators	Bot-network operators use a network, or bot-net, of compromised, remotely controlled systems to coordinate attacks and to distribute phishing schemes, spam, and malware attacks. The services of these networks are sometimes made available on underground markets (e.g., purchasing a denial-of-service attack or services to relay spam or phishing attacks).
Criminal groups	Criminal groups seek to attack systems for monetary gain. Specifically, organized criminal groups use spam, phishing, and spyware/malware to commit identity theft, online fraud, and computer extortion. International corporate spies and criminal organizations also pose a threat to the United States through their ability to conduct industrial espionage and large-scale monetary theft and to hire or develop hacker talent.
Hackers	Hackers break into networks for the thrill of the challenge, bragging rights in the hacker community, revenge, stalking, monetary gain, and political activism, among other reasons. While gaining unauthorized access once required a fair amount of skill or computer knowledge, hackers can now download attack scripts and protocols from the Internet and launch them against victim sites. Thus, while attack tools have become more sophisticated, they have also become easier to use. According to the Central Intelligence Agency, the large majority of hackers do not have the requisite expertise to threaten difficult targets such as critical U.S. networks. Nevertheless, the worldwide population of hackers poses a relatively high threat of an isolated or brief disruption causing serious damage.
Insiders	The disgruntled organization insider is a principal source of computer crime. Insiders may not need a great deal of knowledge about computer intrusions because their knowledge of a target system often allows them to gain unrestricted access to cause damage to the system or to steal system data. The insider threat includes contractors hired by the organization, as well as careless or poorly trained employees who may inadvertently introduce malware into systems.
Nations	Nations use cyber tools as part of their information-gathering and espionage activities. In addition, several nations are aggressively working to develop information warfare doctrine, programs, and capabilities. Such capabilities enable a single entity to have a significant and serious impact by disrupting the supply, communications, and economic infrastructures that support military power—impacts that could affect the daily lives of citizens across the country. In his January 2012 testimony,

Table 1. (Continued)

Threat source	Description
	the Director of National Intelligence stated that, among state actors,China and Russia are of particular concern.
Phishers	Individuals or small groups execute phishing schemes in an attempt to steal identities or information for monetary gain. Phishers may also use spam and spyware or malware to accomplish their objectives.
Spammers	Individuals or organizations distribute unsolicited e-mail with hidden or false information in order to sell products, conduct phishing schemes, distribute spyware or malware, or attack organizations (e.g., a denial of service).
Spyware or malware authors	Individuals or organizations with malicious intent carry out attacks against users by producing and distributing spyware and malware. Several destructive viruses and worms have harmed files and hard drives, and reportedly have even caused physical damage to critical infrastructure, including the Melissa Macro Virus, the Explore.Zip worm, the CIH (Chernobyl) Virus, Nimda, and Code Red.
Terrorists	Terrorists seek to destroy, incapacitate, or exploit critical infrastructures in order to threaten national security, cause mass casualties, weaken the economy, and damage public morale and confidence. Terrorists may use phishing schemes or spyware/malware in order to generate funds or gather sensitive

Source: GAO analysis based on data from the Director of National Intelligence, Department of Justice, Central Intelligence Agency, and the Software Engineering Institute's CERT® Coordination Center.

- Threats to national security include those aimed against the systems and networks of the U.S. government, including the U.S. military, as well as private companies that support government activities or control critical infrastructure. These threats may be intended to cause harm for monetary gain or political or military advantage and can result, among other things, in the disclosure of classified information or the disruption of operations supporting critical infrastructure, national defense, or emergency services.
- Threats to commerce and intellectual property include those aimed at obtaining the confidential intellectual property of private companies, the U.S. government, or individuals with the aim of using that intellectual property for economic gain. For example, product specifications may be stolen to facilitate counterfeiting and piracy or

to gain a competitive edge over a commercial rival. In some cases, theft of intellectual property may also have national security repercussions, as when designs for weapon systems are compromised.

- Threats to individuals include those that lead to the unauthorized disclosure of personally identifiable information, such as taxpayer data, Social Security numbers, credit and debit card information, or medical records. The disclosure of such information could cause harm to individuals, such as identity theft, financial loss, and embarrassment.

The sources of these threats vary in terms of the types and capabilities of the actors, their willingness to act, and their motives. Table 1 shows common sources of adversarial cybersecurity threats.

Table 2. Types of Cyber Attacks

Types of attack	Description
Cross-site scripting	An attack that uses third-party web resources to run a script within the victim's web browser or scriptable application. This occurs when a browser visits a malicious website or clicks a malicious link. The most dangerous consequences occur when this method is used to exploit additional vulnerabilities that may permit an attacker to steal cookies (data exchanged between a web server and a browser), log key strokes, capture screen shots, discover and collect network information, and remotely access and control the victim's machine.
Denial-of-service	An attack that prevents or impairs the authorized use of networks, systems, or applications by exhausting resources.
Distributed denial-of-service	A variant of the denial-of-service attack that uses numerous hosts to perform the attack.
Logic bombs	A piece of programming code intentionally inserted into a software system that will cause a malicious function to occur when one or more specified conditions are met.
Phishing	A digital form of social engineering that uses authentic-looking, but fake, e-mails to request information from users or direct them to a fake website that requests information.
Passive wiretapping	The monitoring or recording of data, such as passwords transmitted in clear text, while they are being transmitted over a communications link. This is done without altering or affecting the data.

Table 2. (Continued)

Types of attack	Description
Structured Query Language injection	An attack that involves the alteration of a database search in a web-based application, which can be used to obtain unauthorized access to sensitive information in a database.
Trojan horse	A computer program that appears to have a useful function, but also has a hidden and potentially malicious function that evades security mechanisms by, for example, masquerading as a useful program that a user would likely execute.
Virus	A computer program that can copy itself and infect a computer without the permission or knowledge of the user. A virus might corrupt or delete data on a computer, use e-mail programs to spread itself to other computers, or even erase everything on a hard disk. Unlike a worm, a virus requires human involvement (usually unwitting) to propagate.
War driving	The method of driving through cities and neighborhoods with a wireless-equipped computer– sometimes with a powerful antenna–searching for unsecured wireless networks.
Worm	A self-replicating, self-propagating, self-contained program that uses network mechanisms to spread itself. Unlike viruses, worms do not require human involvement to propagate.

Source: GAO analysis of data from the National Institute of Standards and Technology, United States Computer Emergency Readiness Team, and industry reports.

These sources of cybersecurity threats make use of various techniques, or attacks that may compromise information or adversely affect computers, software, a network, an organization's operation, an industry, or the Internet itself. Table 2 provides descriptions of common types of cyber attacks.

The unique nature of cyber-based attacks can vastly enhance their reach and impact, resulting in the loss of sensitive information and damage to economic and national security, the loss of privacy, identity theft, or the compromise of proprietary information or intellectual property. The increasing number of incidents reported by federal agencies, and the recently reported cyber-based attacks against individuals, businesses, critical infrastructures, and government organizations have further underscored the need to manage and bolster the cybersecurity of our government's information systems and our nation's critical infrastructures.

Number of Incidents Reported by Federal Agencies Continues to Rise, and Recently Reported Incidents Illustrate Potential Impact

Federal agencies have reported increasing numbers of cybersecurity incidents that have placed sensitive information at risk, with potentially serious impacts on federal operations, assets, and people. The increasing risks to federal systems are demonstrated by the dramatic increase in reports of security incidents, the ease of obtaining and using hacking tools, and steady advances in the sophistication and effectiveness of attack technology. As shown in figure 1, over the past 6 years, the number of incidents reported by federal agencies to the U.S. Computer Emergency Readiness Team (US-CERT) has increased from 5,503 in fiscal year 2006 to 48,562 incidents in fiscal year 2012, an increase of 782 percent. These incidents include, among others, the installation of malware,[8] improper use of computing resources, and unauthorized access to systems.

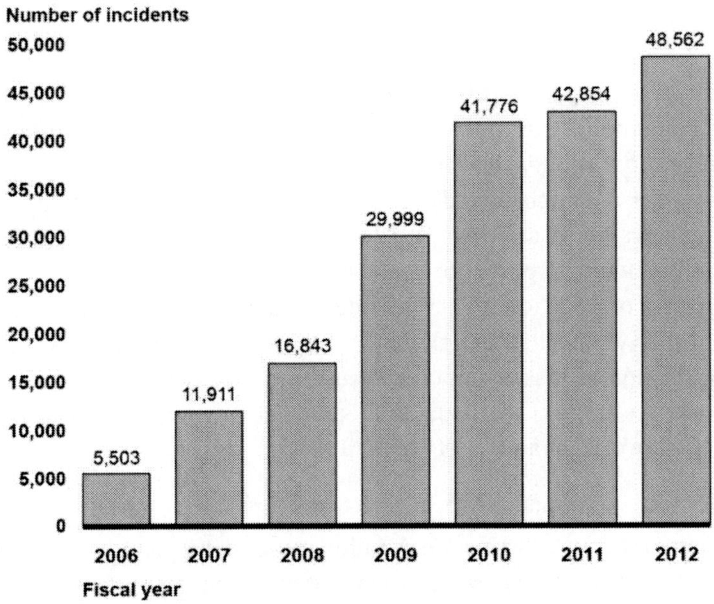

Source: GAO analysis of US-CERT data for fiscal years 2006-2012.

Figure 1. Incidents Reported to US-CERT: Fiscal Years 2006-2012.

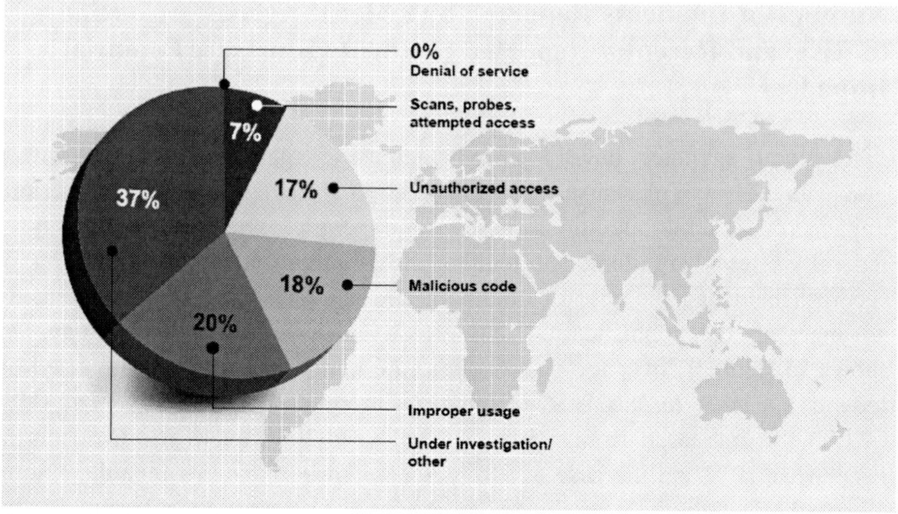

Source: GAO analysis of US-CERT data and GAO reports.

Figure 2. Incidents Reported to US-CERT by Federal Agencies in FY 2012 by Category.

Of the incidents occurring in 2012 (not including those that were reported as under investigation), improper usage,[9] malicious code, and unauthorized access were the most widely reported types across the federal government. As indicated in figure 2, which includes a breakout of incidents reported to US-CERT by agencies in fiscal year 2012, improper usage accounted for 20 percent of total incidents reported by agencies.

In addition, reports of cyber incidents affecting national security, intellectual property, and individuals have been widespread and involve data loss or theft, economic loss, computer intrusions, and privacy breaches. The following examples from news media and other public sources illustrate that a broad array of information and assets remain at risk.

Incidents Affecting National Security

- In February 2012, the National Aeronautics and Space Administration (NASA) inspector general testified that computers with Chinese-based Internet protocol addresses had gained full access to key systems at its Jet Propulsion Laboratory, enabling attackers to modify, copy, or delete sensitive files; create user accounts for mission-critical laboratory systems; and upload hacking tools to steal user credentials and compromise other NASA systems.[10] These individuals were also able to modify system logs to conceal their actions.

- In March 2011, attackers breached the networks of RSA, the Security Division of EMC Corporation,[11] and obtained information about network authentication tokens for a U.S. military contractor. In May 2011, attackers used this information to make duplicate network authentication tokens and breached the contractor's security systems containing sensitive weapons information and military technology. EMC published information about the breach and the immediate steps customers could take to strengthen the security of their systems.
- In 2008, the Department of Defense was successfully compromised when an infected flash drive was inserted into a U.S. military laptop at a military base in the Middle East. The flash drive contained malicious computer code, placed there by a foreign intelligence agency, that uploaded itself onto the military network, spreading through classified and unclassified systems. According to the then Deputy Secretary of Defense, this incident was the most significant breach of U.S. military computers at that time, and DOD's subsequent *Strategy for Operating in Cyberspace* was designed in part to prevent such attacks from recurring in the future.

Incidents Affecting Commerce and Intellectual Property

- In March 2011, an individual was found guilty of distributing source code stolen from his employer, an American company. The investigation revealed that a Chinese company paid the individual $1.5 million to create control system source code based on the American company's design. The Chinese company stopped the delivery of the turbines from the American company, resulting in revenue loss for the American company.
- In February 2011, media reports stated that computer attackers broke into and stole proprietary information worth millions of dollars from networks of six U.S. and European energy companies.
- In mid-2009, a research chemist with DuPont Corporation downloaded proprietary information to a personal e-mail account and thumb drive with the intention of transferring this information to Peking University in China and also sought Chinese government funding to commercialize research related to the information he had stolen.

Incidents Affecting Individuals

- In May 2012, the Federal Retirement Thrift Investment Board[12] reported a sophisticated cyber attack on the computer of a third party that provided services to the Thrift Savings Plan (TSP).[13] As a result of the attack, approximately 123,000 TSP participants had their personal information accessed. According to the board, the information included 43,587 individuals' names, addresses, and Social Security numbers; and 79,614 individuals' Social Security numbers and other TSP-related information.
- In March 2012, attackers breached a server that held thousands of Medicaid records at the Utah Department of Health. Included in the breach were the names of Medicaid recipients and clients of the Children's Health Insurance Plan. In addition, approximately 280,000 people had their Social Security numbers exposed, and another 350,000 people listed in the eligibility inquiries may have had other sensitive data stolen, including names, birth dates, and addresses.
- In March 2012, Global Payments, a credit-transaction processor in Atlanta, reported a data breach that exposed credit and debit card account information of as many as 1.5 million accounts in North America. Although Global Payments does not believe any personal information was taken, it provided alerts and planned to pay for credit monitoring for those whose personal information was at risk.

These incidents illustrate the serious impact that cyber attacks can have on federal and military operations, critical infrastructure, and the confidentiality, integrity, and availability of sensitive government, private sector, and personal information.

Federal Information Security Responsibilities Are Established in Law and Policy

Federal law and policy address agency responsibilities for cybersecurity in a variety of ways, reflecting its complexity and the nature of our country's political and economic structure. Requirements for securing the federal government's information systems are addressed in federal laws and policies. Beyond high-level critical infrastructure protection responsibilities, the existence of a federal role in securing systems not controlled by the federal government typically relates to the government's application of regulatory authority and reflects the fact that much of our nation's economic infrastructure is owned and controlled by the private sector. Certain federal agencies have cybersecurity-related responsibilities within a specific economic sector and may issue standards and guidance. For example, the Federal Energy Regulatory Commission approves cybersecurity standards in carrying out responsibilities for the reliability of the nation's bulk power system. In sectors where the use of federal cybersecurity guidance is not mandatory, entities may voluntarily implement such guidance in response to business incentives, including to mitigate risks, protect intellectual property, ensure interoperability among systems, and encourage the use of leading practices.

The Federal Information Security Management Act of 2002 (FISMA)[14] sets forth a comprehensive risk-based framework for ensuring the effectiveness of information security controls over information resources that support federal operations and assets. In order to ensure the implementation of this framework, FISMA assigns specific responsibilities to agencies, OMB, NIST, and inspectors general.

FISMA requires each agency to develop, document, and implement an information security program to include, among other things,

- periodic assessments of the risk and magnitude of harm that could result from the unauthorized access, use, disclosure, disruption, modification, or destruction of information or information systems;
- policies and procedures that (1) are based on risk assessments, (2) cost-effectively reduce information security risks to an acceptable level, (3) ensure that information security is addressed throughout the life cycle of each system, and (4) ensure compliance with applicable requirements;
- security awareness training to inform personnel of information security risks and of their responsibilities in complying with agency policies and procedures, as well as training personnel with significant security responsibilities for information security;
- periodic testing and evaluation of the effectiveness of information security policies, procedures, and practices, to be performed with a frequency depending on risk, but no less than annually, and that includes testing of management, operational, and technical controls for every system identified in the agency's required inventory of major information systems; and
- procedures for detecting, reporting, and responding to security incidents.

In addition, FISMA requires each agency to report annually to OMB, selected congressional committees, and the U.S. Comptroller General on the adequacy of its information security policies, procedures, practices, and compliance with requirements.

OMB's responsibilities include developing and overseeing the implementation of policies, principles, standards, and guidelines on information security in federal agencies (except with regard to national security systems[15]). It is also responsible for reviewing, at least annually, and approving or disapproving agency information security programs.

NIST's responsibilities under FISMA include the development of security standards and guidelines for agencies that include standards for categorizing information and information systems according to ranges of risk levels, minimum security requirements for information and information systems in risk categories, guidelines for detection and handling of information security incidents, and guidelines for identifying an information system as a national security system (NIST standards and guidelines, like OMB policies, do not apply to national security systems[16]). NIST also has related responsibilities under the Cyber Security Research and Development Act that include developing a checklist of settings and option selections to minimize security risks associated with computer hardware and software widely used within the federal government.[17]

FISMA also requires each agency inspector general to annually evaluate the information security program and practices of the agency. The results of these evaluations are submitted to OMB, and OMB is to summarize the results in its reporting to Congress.

In the 10 years since FISMA was enacted into law, executive branch oversight of agency information security has changed. As part of its FISMA oversight responsibilities, OMB has issued annual guidance to agencies on implementing FISMA requirements, including instructions for agency and inspector general reporting. However, in July 2010, the Director of OMB and the White House Cybersecurity Coordinator[18] issued a joint memorandum[19] stating that DHS was to exercise primary responsibility within the executive branch for the operational aspects of cybersecurity for federal information systems that fall within the scope of FISMA. The memo stated that DHS activities would include five specific responsibilities of OMB under FISMA:

- overseeing implementation of and reporting on government cybersecurity policies and guidance;

- overseeing and assisting government efforts to provide adequate, risk-based, and cost-effective cybersecurity;
- overseeing agencies' compliance with FISMA;
- overseeing agencies' cybersecurity operations and incident response; and
- annually reviewing agencies' cybersecurity programs.[20]

The OMB memo also stated that in carrying out these responsibilities, DHS is to be subject to general OMB oversight in accordance with the provisions of FISMA. In addition, the memo stated that the Cybersecurity Coordinator would lead the interagency process for cybersecurity strategy and policy development. Subsequent to the issuance of M-10-28, DHS began issuing annual reporting instructions to agencies in addition to OMB's annual guidance.[21]

In addition to FISMA's information security program provisions, federal agencies operating national security systems must also comply with requirements for enhanced protections for those sensitive systems. National Security Directive 42 established the Committee on National Security Systems, an organization chaired by the Department of Defense, to, among other things, issue policy directives and instructions that provide mandatory information security requirements for national security systems.[22] In addition, the defense and intelligence communities develop implementing instructions and may add additional requirements where needed. The Department of Defense also has particular responsibilities for cybersecurity issues related to national defense. To address these issues, DOD has undertaken a number of initiatives, including establishing the U.S. Cyber Command.[23] An effort is underway to harmonize policies and guidance for national security and non-national security systems. Representatives from civilian, defense, and intelligence agencies established a joint task force in 2009, led by NIST and including senior leadership and subject matter experts from participating agencies, to publish common guidance for information systems security for national security and non-national security systems.[24]

Various laws and directives have also given federal agencies responsibilities relating to the protection of critical infrastructures, which are largely owned by private sector organizations.[25] The Homeland Security Act of 2002 created the Department of Homeland Security. Among other things, DHS was assigned with the following critical infrastructure protection responsibilities: (1) developing a comprehensive national plan for securing the critical infrastructures of the United States, (2) recommending measures to protect those critical infrastructures in coordination with other groups, and (3) disseminating, as appropriate, information to assist in the deterrence, prevention, and preemption of, or response to, terrorist attacks.

Homeland Security Presidential Directive 7 (HSPD-7) was issued in December 2003 and defined additional responsibilities for DHS, sector-specific agencies,[26] and other departments and agencies. The directive instructs sector-specific agencies to collaborate with the private sector to identify, prioritize, and coordinate the protection of critical infrastructures to prevent, deter, and mitigate the effects of attacks. It also makes DHS responsible for, among other things, coordinating national critical infrastructure protection efforts and establishing uniform policies, approaches, guidelines, and methodologies for integrating federal infrastructure protection and risk management activities within and across sectors.

The recently concluded 112th Congress considered enacting new legislation to address federal information security oversight responsibilities. For example, the Cybersecurity Act of 2012, S. 3414, which was endorsed by the Obama administration with its July 26, 2012, Statement of Administration Policy, proposed to amend FISMA to give OMB's statutory oversight responsibilities to DHS.[27] The SECURE IT Act, S. 3342, would have given the Department of Commerce that oversight responsibility in consultation with DHS.[28] The Federal Information Security Amendments Act of 2012, H.R. 4257, proposed to preserve OMB's FISMA oversight duties. The Executive Cyberspace Coordination Act of 2011, H.R. 1136, would have given OMB's role to a newly created National Office for Cyberspace in the Executive Office of the President.[29] While H.R. 4257 was passed by the House of Representatives, none of these bills were enacted into law during the recently completed 112th Congress.

Strategic Approaches to Cybersecurity Can Help Organizations Focus on Objectives

Implementing a comprehensive strategic approach to cybersecurity requires the development of strategy documents to guide the activities that will support this approach. These strategy documents are starting points that define the problems and risks intended to be addressed by organizations as well as plans for tackling those problems and risks, allocating and managing the appropriate resources, identifying different organizations' roles and responsibilities, and linking (or integrating) all planned actions.

As envisioned by the Government Performance and Results Act (GPRA) of 1993,[30] developing a strategic plan can help clarify organizational priorities and unify employees in the pursuit of shared goals.

Such a plan can be of particular value in linking long-term performance goals and objectives horizontally across multiple organizations. In addition, it provides a basis for integrating, rather than merely coordinating, a wide array of activities.

If done well, strategic planning is continuous and provides the basis for the important activities an organization does each day, moving it closer to accomplishing its ultimate objectives. By more closely aligning its activities, processes, and resources with its goals, the government can be better positioned to accomplish those goals.

Federal Strategy Has Evolved Over Time but Is Not Fully Defined

Although the federal strategy to address cybersecurity issues has been described in a number of documents, no integrated, overarching strategy has been developed that synthesizes these documents to provide a comprehensive description of the current strategy, including priority actions, responsibilities for performing them, and time frames for their completion. Existing strategy documents have not always addressed key elements of the desirable characteristics of a strategic approach.

Among the items generally not included in cybersecurity strategy documents are mechanisms such as milestones and performance measures, cost and resource allocations, clear delineations of roles and responsibilities, and explanations of how the documents integrate with other national strategies. The items that have generally been missing are key to helping ensure that the vision and priorities outlined in the documents are effectively implemented. Without an overarching strategy that includes such mechanisms, the government is less able to determine the progress it has made in reaching its objectives and to hold key organizations accountable for carrying out planned activities.

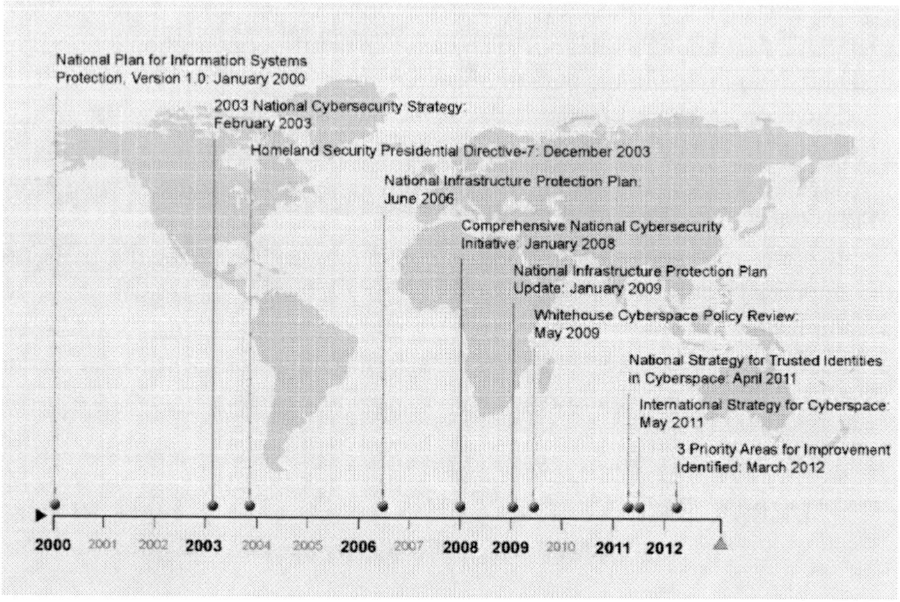

Source: GAO analysis of federal strategy documents.

Figure 3. Evolution of National Strategies Related to Cybersecurity.

Cybersecurity Strategy Documents Have Evolved over Time

There is no single document that comprehensively defines the nation's cybersecurity strategy. Instead, various documents developed over the span of more than a decade have contributed to the national strategy, often revising priorities due to changing circumstances or assigning new responsibilities to various organizations. The evolution of the nation's cybersecurity strategy is summarized in figure 3.

The major cybersecurity initiatives and strategy documents that have been developed over the last 12 years are discussed below.

The National Plan for Information Systems Protection

In 2000, President Clinton issued the *National Plan for Information Systems Protection*. The plan was intended as a first major element of a more comprehensive effort to protect the nation's information systems and critical assets from future attacks. It focused on federal efforts to protect the nation's critical cyber-based infrastructures. It identified risks associated with our nation's dependence on computers and networks for critical services;

recognized the need for the federal government to take a lead role in addressing critical infrastructure risks; and outlined key concepts and general initiatives to assist in achieving its goals. The plan identified specific action items and milestones for 10 component programs that were aimed at addressing the need to prepare for and prevent cyber attacks, detect and respond to attacks when they occur, and build strong foundations to support these efforts.

The National Strategy to Secure Cyberspace

In 2003, the *National Strategy to Secure Cyberspace* was released. It was also intended to provide a framework for organizing and prioritizing efforts to protect cyberspace and was organized according to five national priorities, with major actions and initiatives identified for each. These priorities were

- a National Cyberspace Security Response System,
- a National Cyberspace Security Threat and Vulnerability Reduction Program,
- a National Cyberspace Security Awareness and Training Program,
- Securing Governments' Cyberspace, and
- National Security and International Cyberspace Security Cooperation.

In describing the threats to and vulnerabilities of cyberspace, the strategy highlighted the potential for damage to U.S. information systems from attacks by terrorist organizations.

Although it is unclear whether the 2003 strategy replaced the 2000 plan or was meant to be a supplemental document, the priorities of the 2003 strategy are similar to those of the 2000 document. For example, the 2003 strategy's priority of establishing a national cyberspace security threat and vulnerability reduction program aligns with the 2000 plan's programs related to identifying critical infrastructure assets and shared interdependencies, addressing vulnerabilities, and detecting attacks and unauthorized intrusions. In addition, the 2003 strategy's priority of minimizing damage and recovery time from cyber attacks aligns with the 2000 plan's program related to creating capabilities for response, reconstitution, and recovery. The 2000 plan also included programs addressing awareness and training, cyber-related counterintelligence and law enforcement, international cooperation, and research and development, similar to the 2003 strategy.

The Comprehensive National Cybersecurity Initiative

In 2008, President Bush issued National Security Presidential Directive 54/Homeland Security Presidential Directive 23, establishing the *Comprehensive National Cybersecurity Initiative* (CNCI), a set of 12 projects aimed at safeguarding executive branch information systems by reducing potential vulnerabilities, protecting against intrusion attempts, and anticipating future threats. The 12 projects were the following:

1. **Trusted Internet Connections:** Reduce and consolidate external access points with the goal of limiting points of access to the Internet for executive branch civilian agencies.
2. **EINSTEIN 2:** Deploy passive sensors across executive branch civilian systems that have the ability to scan the content of Internet packets to determine whether they contain malicious code.
3. **EINSTEIN 3:** Pursue deployment of an intrusion prevention system that will allow for real-time prevention capabilities that will assess and block harmful code.
4. **Research and Development Efforts:** Coordinate and redirect research and development (R&D) efforts with a focus on coordinating both classified and unclassified R&D for cybersecurity.
5. **Connecting the Centers:** Connect current cyber centers to enhance cyber situational awareness and lead to greater integration and understanding of the cyber threat.
6. **Cyber Counterintelligence Plan:** Develop a government-wide cyber counterintelligence plan by improving the security of the physical and electromagnetic integrity of U.S. networks.
7. **Security of Classified Networks:** Increase the security of classified networks to reduce the risk of information they contain being disclosed.
8. **Expand Education:** Expand education efforts by constructing a comprehensive federal cyber education and training program, with attention to offensive and defensive skills and capabilities.
9. **Leap-Ahead Technology:** Define and develop enduring leap-ahead technology, strategies, and programs by investing in high-risk, high-reward research and development and by working with both private sector and international partners.
10. **Deterrence Strategies and Programs:** Define and develop enduring deterrence strategies and programs that focus on reducing vulnerabilities and deter interference and attacks in cyberspace.

11. **Global Supply Chain Risk Management:** Develop a multipronged approach for global supply chain risk management while seeking to better manage the federal government's global supply chain.
12. **Public and Private Partnerships "Project 12":** Define the federal role for extending cyber security into critical infrastructure domains and seek to define new mechanisms for the federal government and industry to work together to protect the nation's critical infrastructure.

The CNCI's projects are generally consistent with both the 2000 strategy and the 2003 strategy, while also introducing new priorities. For example, all three strategy documents address counterintelligence, education and awareness, research and development, reducing vulnerabilities, and public-private partnerships. However, the CNCI introduces additional priorities for the security of classified networks and global supply chain risk management, and it does not include programs to address response, reconstitution, and recovery or international cooperation, as in the previous strategies.

White House Cyberspace Policy Review

Shortly after taking office in 2009, President Obama ordered a thorough review of the federal government's efforts to defend the nation's information and communications infrastructure as well as the development of a comprehensive approach to cybersecurity. The White House *Cyberspace Policy Review*, released in May 2009, was the result. It recommended that the President appoint a national cybersecurity coordinator, which was completed in December 2009. It also recommended, among many other things, that a coherent unified policy guidance be developed that clarifies roles, responsibilities, and the application of agency authorities for cybersecurity-related activities across the federal government; a cybersecurity incident response plan be prepared; a national public awareness and education campaign be initiated that promotes cybersecurity; and a framework for research and development strategies be created. According to the policy review, President Obama determined that the CNCI and its associated activities should evolve to become key elements of a broader, updated national strategy. In addition, the CNCI initiatives were to play a key role in supporting the achievement of many of the policy review's recommendations.

National Strategy for Trusted Identities in Cyberspace

The National Strategy for Trusted Identities in Cyberspace[31] is one of several strategy documents that are subordinate to the government's overall cybersecurity strategy and focuses on specific areas of concern. Specifically, this strategy aims at improving the security of online transactions by strengthening the way identities are established and confirmed. The strategy envisions secure, efficient, easy-to-use, and interoperable identity solutions to access online services in a manner that promotes confidence, privacy, choice, and innovation. In order to fulfill its vision, the strategy calls for

- developing a comprehensive Identity Ecosystem[32] Framework,
- building and implementing interoperable identity solutions,
- enhancing confidence and willingness to participate in the Identity Ecosystem, and
- ensuring the long-term success and viability of the Identity Ecosystem.

The first two goals focus on designing and building the necessary policy and technology to deliver trusted online services. The third goal encourages adoption, including the use of education and awareness efforts. The fourth goal promotes the continued development and enhancement of the Identity Ecosystem. For each goal, there are objectives that enable the achievement of the goal by addressing barriers in the current environment. The strategy states that these goals will require the active collaboration of all levels of government and the private sector. The private sector is seen as the primary developer, implementer, owner, and operator of the Identity Ecosystem, and the federal government's role is to "enable" the private sector and lead by example through the early adoption and provision of Identity Ecosystem services.

Strategic Plan for Cybersecurity Research and Development

In response to the R&D-related recommendations in the White House *Cyberspace Policy Review*, the Office of Science and Technology Policy (OSTP)[33] issued the first cybersecurity R&D strategic plan[34] in December 2011, which defines a set of interrelated priorities for government agencies conducting or sponsoring cybersecurity R&D. This document is another of the subordinate strategy documents that address specific areas of concern. The priorities defined in the plan are organized into four goals—inducing change, developing scientific foundations, maximizing research impact, and accelerating transition to practice—that are aimed at limiting current cyberspace deficiencies, precluding future problems, and expediting the infusion of research accomplishments in the marketplace. Specifically, the plan identifies what research is needed to reduce cyber attacks. It includes the following themes:

- building a secure software system that is resilient to attacks;
- supporting security policies and security services for different types of cyberspace interactions;
- deploying systems that are both diverse and changing, to increase complexity and costs for attackers and system resiliency; and
- developing cybersecurity incentives to create foundations for cybersecurity markets, establish meaningful metrics, and promote economically sound and secure practices.

International Strategy for Cyberspace

Like the strategies for trusted cyberspace identities and cyberspace R&D, the *International Strategy for Cyberspace*,[35] released by the White House in May 2011, is a subordinate strategy document that addresses a specific area of concern. The International Strategy for Cyberspace is intended to be a roadmap for better definition and coordination of U.S. international cyberspace policy. According to the strategy, in order to reach the goal of working internationally to promote an open, interoperable, secure, and reliable information and communications infrastructure, the government is to build and sustain an environment in which norms of responsible behavior guide states' actions, sustain partnerships, and support the rule of law in cyberspace. The strategy stated that these cyberspace norms should be supported by principles such as upholding fundamental freedoms, respect for property, valuing privacy, protection from crime, and the right of self-defense. The strategy also included seven interdependent focus areas:

1. Economy: Promoting International Standards and Innovative, Open Markets.
2. Protecting our Networks: Enhancing Security Reliability and Resiliency.
3. Law Enforcement: Extending Collaboration and the Rule of Law.
4. Military: Preparing for 21st Century Security Challenges.
5. Internet Governance: Promoting Effective and Inclusive Structures.
6. International Development: Building Capacity, Security, and Prosperity.
7. Internet Freedom: Supporting Fundamental Freedoms and Privacy.

2012 Cross-Agency Priority Goals

In a March 2012 blog post, the White House Cybersecurity Coordinator announced that his office, in coordination with experts from DHS, DOD, NIST, and OMB, had identified three priority areas for improvement within federal cybersecurity:

- **Trusted Internet connections:** Consolidate external telecommunication connections and ensure a set of baseline security capabilities for situational awareness and enhanced monitoring.
- **Continuous monitoring of federal information systems:** Transform the otherwise static security control assessment and authorization process into a dynamic risk mitigation program that provides essential, near real-time security status and remediation, increasing visibility into system operations and helping security personnel make risk management decisions based on increased situational awareness.
- **Strong authentication:** Increase the use of federal smartcard credentials such as Personal Identity Verification and Common Access Cards that provide multifactor authentication and digital signature and encryption capabilities, authorizing users to access federal information systems with a higher level of assurance.

According to the post, these priorities were selected to focus federal department and agency cybersecurity efforts on implementing the most cost-effective and efficient cybersecurity controls for federal information system security. To support the implementation of these priorities, cybersecurity was included among a limited number of cross-agency priority goals, as required to be established under the GPRA Modernization Act of 2010.[36] The cybersecurity goal was to achieve 95 percent use of critical cybersecurity capabilities on federal executive branch information systems by the end of 2014, including the three priorities mentioned above. The White House Cybersecurity Coordinator was designated as the goal leader, but according to one White House website, http://www.performance.gov, DHS was tasked with leading the government-wide coordination efforts to implement the goal. The administration's priorities were included in its fiscal year 2011 FISMA report to Congress. In addition, both OMB and DHS FISMA reporting instructions require federal agencies to report on progress in meeting those priorities in their 2012 FISMA reports.

There are a number of implementation plans aimed at executing various aspects of the national strategy. For example, the *National Infrastructure*

Protection Plan (NIPP)[37] describes DHS's overarching approach for integrating the nation's critical infrastructure protection initiatives in a single effort. The goal of the NIPP is to prevent, deter, neutralize, or mitigate the effects of terrorist attacks on our nation's critical infrastructure and to strengthen national preparedness, timely response, and rapid recovery of critical infrastructure in the event of an attack, natural disaster, or other emergency. The NIPP's objectives include understanding and sharing information about terrorist threats and other hazards with critical infrastructure partners; building partnerships to share information and implement critical infrastructure protection programs; implementing a long-term risk management program; and maximizing the efficient use of resources for critical infrastructure protection, restoration, and recovery.

No Overarching Cybersecurity Strategy Has been Developed

While various subordinate strategies and implementation plans focusing on specific cybersecurity issues have been released in the past few years, no overarching national cybersecurity strategy document has been prepared that synthesizes the relevant portions of these documents or provides a comprehensive description of the current strategy. According to officials at the Executive Office of the President, the current national cybersecurity strategy consists of several documents and statements issued at different times, including the 2003 strategy, which is now almost a decade old, the 2009 White House policy review, and subordinate strategies such as the R&D strategy and the international strategy. Also implicitly included in the national strategy are the modifications made when the CNCI was introduced in 2008 and the 2012 statement regarding cross-agency priority goals.

Despite the fact that no overarching document has been created, the White House has asserted that the national strategy has in fact been updated. We reported in October 2010 that a committee had been formed to prepare an update to the 2003 strategy in response to the recommendation of the 2009 policy review.[38] However, no updated strategy document has been issued. In May 2011, the White House announced that it had completed all the near-term actions outlined in the 2009 policy review, including the update to the 2003 national strategy. According to the administration's fact sheet on cybersecurity accomplishments,[39] the 2009 policy review itself serves as the updated strategy. The fact sheet stated that the direction and needs highlighted in the *Cyberspace Policy Review* and the previous national cybersecurity strategy were still relevant, and it noted that the administration had updated its strategy on two subordinate cyber issues, identity management and international engagement. However, these actions do not fulfill the recommendation that an updated strategy be prepared for the President's approval. As a result, no overarching strategy exists to show how the various goals and activities articulated in current documents form an integrated strategic approach.

Useful Strategies Should Include Desirable Characteristics

In 2004 we identified a set of desirable characteristics that can enhance the usefulness of national strategies as guidance for decision makers in allocating resources, defining policies, and helping to ensure accountability.[40] Table 3 provides a summary of the six characteristics.

Table 3. Summary of Desirable Characteristics for a National Strategy

Desirable characteristic	Description
Purpose, scope, and methodology	Addresses why the strategy was produced, the scope of its coverage, and the process by which it was developed.
Problem definition and risk assessment	Addresses the particular national problems and threats the strategy is directed toward.
Goals, subordinate objectives, activities, and performance measures	Addresses what the strategy is trying to achieve and steps to achieve those results, as well as the priorities, milestones, and performance measures to gauge results.
Resources, investments, and risk management	Addresses what implementation of the strategy will cost, the sources and types of resources and investments needed, and where resources and investments should be targeted based on balancing risk reductions with costs.
Organizational roles, responsibilities, and coordination	Addresses who will be implementing the strategy, what their roles will be compared to others, and mechanisms for them to coordinate their efforts.
Linkage to other strategies and implementation	Addresses how a national strategy relates to other strategies' goals, objectives, and activities, and to subordinate levels of government and their plans to implement the strategy.

Source: GAO.

We believe that including all the key elements of these characteristics in a national strategy would provide valuable direction to responsible parties for developing and implementing the strategy, enhance its usefulness as guidance for resource and policy decision makers, and better ensure accountability.

Federal Cybersecurity Strategy Documents Have Not Always Included Key Elements of Desirable Characteristics

The government's cybersecurity strategy documents have generally addressed several of the desirable characteristics of national strategies, but lacked certain key elements. For example, the 2009 White House *Cyberspace Policy Review,* the *Strategy for Trusted Identities in Cyberspace*, and the *Strategic Plan for the Federal Cybersecurity Research and Development Program* addressed purpose, scope, and methodology. In addition, all the documents included the problem definition aspect of "problem definition and risk assessment." Likewise, the documents all generally included goals, subordinate objectives, and activities, which are key elements of the "goals, subordinate objectives, activities, and performance measures" characteristic. However, certain elements of the characteristics were missing from most, if not all, of the documents we reviewed. The key elements that were generally missing from these documents include (1) milestones and performance measures, (2) cost and resources, (3) roles and responsibilities, and (4) linkage with other strategy documents.

Milestones and Performance Measures

Milestones and performance measures were generally not included in strategy documents, appearing only in limited circumstances within subordinate strategies and initiatives. For example, the Cross-Agency Priority Goals for Cybersecurity and the *National Strategy for Trusted Identities in Cyberspace*,[41] which represent only a portion of the national strategy, included milestones for achieving their goals. In addition, the progress in implementing the Cross-Agency Priority Goals for Cybersecurity is tracked through FISMA reports submitted by agencies and their inspectors general. However, in general, the documents and initiatives that currently contribute to the government's overall cybersecurity strategy do not include milestones or performance measures for tracking progress in accomplishing stated goals and objectives. For example, the 2003 *National Strategy to Secure Cyberspace* included no milestones or performance measures for addressing the five priority areas it defined. Likewise, other documents generally did not include either milestones for implementation of the strategy or outcome-related performance measures to gauge success.

The lack of milestones and performance measures at the strategic level is mirrored in similar shortcomings within key government programs that are part of the government-wide strategy. For example, the DHS inspector general reported in 2011 that the DHS Cybersecurity and Communications (CS&C) office had not yet developed objective, quantifiable performance measures to determine whether it was meeting its mission to secure cyberspace and protect critical infrastructures.[42] Additionally, the inspector general reported that CS&C was not able to track its progress efficiently and effectively in addressing the actions outlined in the 2003 *National Cybersecurity Strategy* or achieving the goals outlined in the NIPP. Accordingly, the inspector general recommended that CS&C develop and implement performance measures to be used to track and evaluate the effectiveness of actions defined in its strategic implementation plan. The inspector general also recommended that management use these measures to assess CS&C's overall progress in attaining its strategic goals and milestones. DHS officials stated that, as of January 2012, CS&C had not yet developed objective performance criteria and measures, and that development of these will begin once the CS&C strategic implementation plan is completed.

Many of the experts we consulted cited a lack of accountability as one of the root causes for the slow progress in implementing the nation's cybersecurity goals and objectives. Specifically, cybersecurity and information management experts stated that the inability of the federal government to make progress in addressing persistent weaknesses within its risk-based security framework can be associated with the lack of performance measures and monitoring to assess whether security objectives are being achieved. Without establishing milestones or performance measures in its national strategy, the government lacks a means to ensure priority goals and objectives are accomplished and responsible parties are held accountable.

Cost and Resources

Though the 2000 plan and the 2003 strategy linked some investments to the annual budget, the strategy documents generally did not include an analysis of the cost of planned activities or the source and type of resources needed to carry out the strategy's goals and objectives. The 2000 *National Plan for Information Systems Protection* identified resources for certain cybersecurity activities, and the 2003 *National Strategy to Secure Cyberspace* linked some of its investment requests— such as completing a cyber incident warning system—to the fiscal 2003 budget. However, none of the strategies included an analysis of the cost and resources needed to implement the entire strategy. For example, while the cybersecurity R&D strategic plan mentioned specific initiatives, such as a Defense Advanced Research Projects Agency program to fund biologically inspired cyber-attack resilience, it did not describe how decisions were made regarding the amount of resources to be invested in this or any other R&D initiative. The plan also did not outline how the chosen cybersecurity R&D efforts would be funded and sustained in the future.

In addition, the strategies did not include a business case for investing in activities to support their goals and objectives based on assessments of the risks and relative costs of mitigating them. Many of the private sector experts we consulted stated that not establishing such a value proposition makes it difficult to mobilize the resources needed to significantly improve security within the government as well as to build support in the private sector for a national commitment to cybersecurity. A convincing assessment of the specific risks and resources needed to mitigate them would help implementing parties allocate resources and investments according to priorities and constraints, track costs and performance, and shift existing investments and resources as needed to align with national priorities.

Roles and Responsibilities

Most of the strategies lacked clearly defined roles and responsibilities for key agencies, such as DHS, DOD, and OMB, that contribute substantially to the nation's cybersecurity programs. For example, as already discussed, while the law gives OMB responsibility for oversight of federal government information security, OMB transferred several of its oversight responsibilities to DHS. According to OMB representatives, the oversight responsibilities transferred to DHS represent the operational aspects of its role, in contrast to the general oversight responsibilities stipulated by FISMA, which OMB retained. The representatives further stated that the enlistment of DHS to assist OMB in performing these responsibilities has allowed OMB to have more visibility into the cybersecurity activities of federal agencies because of the additional resources and expertise provided by DHS and that OMB and DHS continue to work closely together. While OMB's decision to transfer several of its responsibilities to DHS may have had beneficial practical results, such as leveraging the resources of DHS, it is not consistent with FISMA, which assigns all of these responsibilities to OMB.

With these responsibilities now divided between the two organizations, it is also unclear how OMB and DHS are to share oversight of individual departments and agencies, which are responsible under FISMA for ensuring the security of their information systems and networks. For example, both DHS and OMB have issued annual FISMA reporting instructions to agencies, which could create confusion among agency officials. Further, the instructions vary in content. In its 2012 instructions, DHS included, among other things, specific actions agencies were required to complete, time frames for completing the actions, and reporting metrics. However, the OMB instructions, although identically titled, included different directions. Specifically, the OMB instructions required agencies to submit metrics data for the first quarter of the fiscal year, while the DHS reporting instructions stated that agencies were not required to submit such data. Further, the OMB instructions stated that agency chief information officers would submit monthly data feeds through the FISMA reporting system, while the DHS instructions indicated that inspectors general and senior agency officials for privacy would also submit monthly data feeds. Issuing identically titled reporting instructions with varying content could result in inconsistent reporting.

Further, it is unclear which agency currently has the role of ensuring that agencies are held accountable for implementing the provisions of FISMA. Although FISMA requires OMB to approve or disapprove agencies' information security programs, OMB has not made explicit statements that would indicate whether an agency's information security program has been approved or disapproved. As a result, a mechanism for establishing accountability and holding agencies accountable for implementing effective programs is not being used.

Mirroring these shortcomings, several GAO reports have likewise demonstrated that the roles and responsibilities of key agencies charged with protecting the nation's cyber assets are inadequately defined. For example, as described in our recent report on gaps in homeland defense and civil support guidance,[43] although DOD has prepared guidance regarding support for civilian agencies in a domestic cyber incident and has an agreement with DHS for preparing for and responding to such incidents, these documents do not clarify all key aspects of how DOD will support a response to a domestic cyber incident. For example, the chartering directives for the Offices of the Assistant Secretary of Defense for Global Strategic Affairs and the Assistant Secretary of Defense for Homeland Defense and Americas' Security Affairs[44] assign overlapping roles and responsibilities for preparing for and responding to domestic cyber incidents. In an October 2012 report, we recommended that DOD update guidance on preparing for and responding to domestic cyber incidents to align with national-level guidance and that such guidance should include a description of DOD's roles and responsibilities. Further, in a March 2010 report on the CNCI,[45] we stated that federal agencies had overlapping and uncoordinated responsibilities and it was unclear where overall responsibility for coordination lay. We recommended that the Director of OMB better define roles and responsibilities for all key CNCI participants to ensure that essential government-wide cybersecurity activities are fully coordinated.

Many of the experts we consulted agreed that the roles and responsibilities of key agencies are not well defined. Clearly defining roles and responsibilities for agencies charged with implementing key aspects of the national cybersecurity strategies would aid in fostering coordination, particularly where there is overlap, and thus enhance both implementation and accountability.

Linkage with Other Key Strategy Documents

The cybersecurity strategy documents we reviewed did not include any discussion of how they linked to or superseded other documents, nor did they describe how they fit into the overall national cybersecurity strategy. For example, the 2003 *National Strategy to Secure Cyberspace* does not refer to the 2000 plan nor describe progress made since the previous strategy was issued or if it was meant to replace or enhance the previous strategy. Each of the subsequent documents that have addressed aspects of the federal government's approach to cybersecurity—such as the *Comprehensive National Cybersecurity Initiative*, the N*ational Strategy for Trusted Identities in Cyberspace*, and the *International Strategy to Secure Cyberspace*—has established its own set of goals and priority actions, but none of these cybersecurity agendas are linked to each other to explain why planned activities differ or are prioritized differently. For example, in 2012, the administration determined that trusted Internet connections, continuous monitoring, and strong authentication should be cross-agency priorities, but no explanation was given as to how these three relate to priorities established in other strategy documents. Specifying how new documents are linked with the overall national cybersecurity strategy would clarify priorities and better establish roles and responsibilities, thereby fostering effective implementation and accountability.

The importance of developing an overarching strategy that links component documents and addresses all key elements was confirmed by our discussions with experts. For example, experts agreed that a strategy should define milestones for achieving specific outcomes and that it should be linked to accountability and execution with performance measures to help in determining whether progress is being made. Without addressing these key elements, the national cybersecurity strategy remains poorly defined and faces many implementation challenges. Until an overarching strategy is developed that addresses these elements, progress in cybersecurity may remain limited and difficult to determine.

THE FEDERAL GOVERNMENT CONTINUES TO FACE CHALLENGES IN IMPLEMENTING CYBERSECURITY THAT COULD BE ADDRESSED BY AN EFFECTIVE STRATEGY

As demonstrated in our reviews and the reviews of inspectors general, the government continues to face cybersecurity implementation challenges in a number of key areas, including those related to protecting our nation's critical infrastructure. For example, audits of federal agencies have found that weaknesses in risk-based management and implementation of controls have not substantially improved over the last 4 years. Incident response capabilities, while becoming more sophisticated, also face persistent challenges in sharing information and developing analytical capability. Challenges likewise remain in developing effective initiatives for promoting education and awareness, coordinating research and development, and interacting with foreign governments and other international entities. Until steps are taken to address these persistent challenges, overall progress in improving the nation's cybersecurity posture is likely to remain limited.

Federal Agencies Face Challenges in Designing and Implementing Risk- based Programs

Developing, implementing, and maintaining security controls is key to preventing successful attacks on computer systems and ensuring that information and systems are not compromised. Ineffective implementation of security controls can result in significant risks, including

- loss or theft of resources, including money and intellectual property;
- inappropriate access to and disclosure, modification, or destruction of sensitive information;
- use of computer resources for unauthorized purposes or to launch attacks on other computer systems;
- damage to networks and equipment;
- loss of business due to lack of customer confidence; and
- increased costs from remediation.

From a strategic perspective, it is important that effective processes be instituted for determining which controls to apply, ensuring they are properly implemented, and measuring their effectiveness. Such processes are core elements of an effective cybersecurity strategy.

Federal Strategies and Guidance Reflect a Risk-based Approach

Federal strategy documents reflect the risk-based approach to managing information security controls established by FISMA and federal guidance. For example, the 2003 *National Strategy to Secure Cyberspace* recognizes the importance of managing risk responsibly and enhancing the nation's ability to minimize the damage that results from successful attacks. It encourages the use of commercially available automated auditing and reporting tools to validate the effectiveness of security controls, and states that these tools are essential to continuously understanding the risks to information systems. While acknowledging the importance of these principles, the 2003 strategy document did not indicate time frames or milestones for accomplishing specific actions or establish measures to determine the progress in achieving those actions.

The 2009 White House *Cyberspace Policy Review* provided more specifics, stating that the federal government, along with state, local, and tribal governments and industry, should develop a set of threat scenarios and metrics that all could use for risk management decisions. The DHS *Blueprint for a Secure Cyber Future,*[46] released in November 2011, included reducing exposure to cyber risk as one of its four goals for protecting critical information infrastructure. According to the blueprint, to achieve this goal the department must identify and harden critical information infrastructure through the deployment of appropriate security measures to manage risk to critical systems and assets.

As discussed previously, OMB, in July 2010, issued a memorandum expanding DHS's cybersecurity role in overseeing federal agencies' implementation of FISMA requirements. As part of DHS's responsibilities for FISMA reporting, the Cybersecurity Performance Management Program within DHS annually reviews FISMA data submitted by agencies and inspectors general to, among other things, identify cyber risks across the federal enterprise. This information informs the annual report to Congress.

To assist agencies in identifying risks, NIST has released risk management and assessment guides for information systems.[47] These guides provide a foundation for the development of an effective risk management program, and include the guidance necessary for assessing and mitigating risks identified within information technology systems. Agencies are required to use these guidance documents when identifying risks to their systems. NIST's guide for managing information security risk provides guidance for an integrated, organization-wide program for managing information security risk to organizational operations, organizational assets, individuals, other organizations, and the nation resulting from the operation and use of federal information systems. The guide describes fundamental concepts associated with managing information security risk across an organization, including risk management at various levels, called tiers. According to NIST, risk management is a process that requires organizations to (1) frame risk (i.e., establish the context for risk-based decisions); (2) assess risk; (3) respond to risk once determined; and (4) monitor risk on an ongoing basis. Figure 4 illustrates the risk management process as applied across the tiers—organization, mission/business process, and information system.

Shortcomings Persist in Assessing Risk, Developing and Implementing Controls, and Monitoring Results in the Federal Government

Our audits and the audits of inspectors general have identified many weaknesses in agencies' risk management processes. Numerous recommendations were made to agencies in fiscal years 2011 and 2012 to address these security control weaknesses, which include risk assessment weaknesses, inconsistent application of controls, and weak monitoring controls.

Assessing Risk

According to NIST, risk is determined by identifying potential threats to the organization and vulnerabilities in its systems, determining the likelihood that a particular threat may exploit vulnerabilities, and assessing the resulting impact on the organization's mission, including the effect on sensitive and critical systems and data. These assessments increase an organization's awareness of risk and can generate support for policies and controls that are adopted in response. Such support can help ensure that policies and controls operate as intended. In addition, identifying and assessing information security risks are essential to determining what controls are required.

Agencies' capabilities for performing risk assessments, as required by FISMA, have declined in recent years. According to OMB's fiscal year 2011 report to Congress on FISMA implementation, agency compliance with risk management requirements suffered the largest decline of any FISMA metric between fiscal year 2010 and 2011. Inspectors general for 8 of 22 major agencies reported compliance in 2011, while 13 of 24 inspectors general reported compliance the year before. The following deficiencies were cited most frequently:

- accreditation boundaries for agency systems were not defined (13 of
- 23 agencies),
- specific risks were not sufficiently communicated to appropriate levels of the organization (12 of 23 agencies),
- risks from a mission or business process perspective were not addressed (12 of 23 agencies), and
- security assessment report was not in accordance with government policies (11 of 23 agencies).

Our own analysis of weaknesses reported by inspectors general shows that the number of weaknesses related to the risk assessment process has greatly increased over the last 4 years. In fiscal year 2008 only 3 of the 24 inspectors general reported weaknesses related to assessing risk. In fiscal year 2011, 18 of 24 reported weaknesses in this area. For example, according to a November 2011 inspector general report, one agency did not have a risk management framework in place and had not fully developed risk management procedures, due to budget cuts. Around the same time, another agency's inspector general reported that while risk management procedures at a system-specific level had been implemented, an agency-wide risk management methodology had not been developed. In an October 2011 report on agencies' efforts to implement information security requirements, we reported that of the 24 major agencies, none had fully or effectively implemented an agency-wide information security program.[48] Of those, 18 had shortcomings in the documentation of their security management programs, which establish the framework and activities for assessing risk, developing and implementing effective security procedures, and monitoring the effectiveness of these procedures.

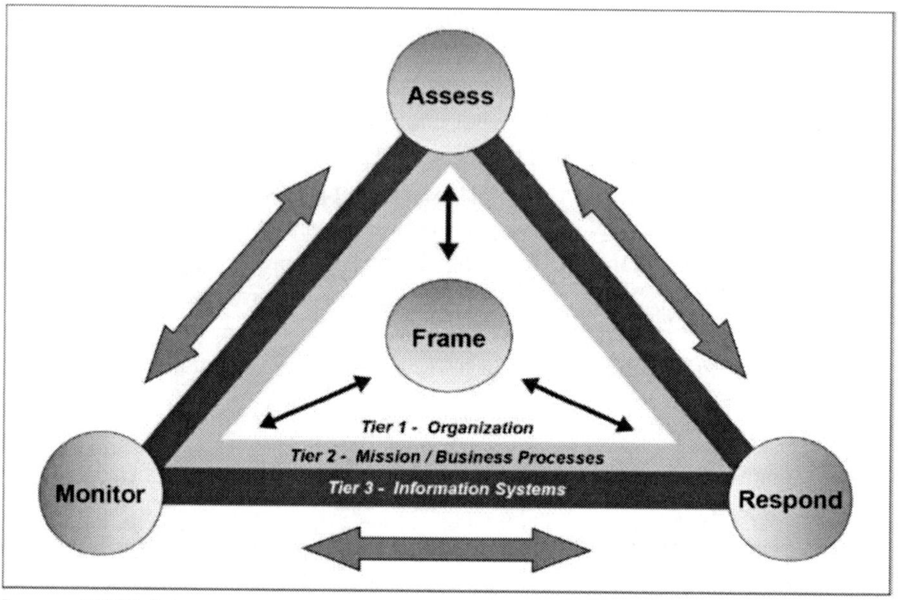

Source: NIST data.

Figure 4. NIST Risk Management Process Applied Across the Tiers.

Risk management was also a topic that our experts felt was very important to a comprehensive approach to cybersecurity. One expert stated that cybersecurity is not a technical problem, but an enterprise- wide risk management challenge that must be tackled in a far more comprehensive manner than is generally understood both at the enterprise and government level. One expert cited defining the cost of insecurity as one of the most significant challenges in improving the nation's cybersecurity posture. Another expert suggested that the risk guidance be reviewed and updated due to changes in technology.

Developing and Implementing Appropriate Controls

NIST has developed guidance to assist agencies, once risks have been assessed, in determining which controls are appropriate for their information and systems. In August 2009, NIST released the third revision of special publication 800-53, *Recommended Security Controls for Federal Information Systems and Organizations*, which provides a catalog of controls and technical guidelines that federal agencies must use to protect federal information and information systems.[49] The use of this NIST guidance for nonfederal information systems, such as those in the nation's critical infrastructure, is encouraged but not required.

Agencies have flexibility in applying NIST guidance, and according to NIST, agencies should apply the security concepts and principles articulated in special publication 800-53 in the context of the agency's missions, business functions, and environment of operation.

In addition, in order to ensure a consistent government-wide baseline, specific guidance has been developed for implementing and configuring controls in certain widely used computing platforms. In fiscal year 2010, DOD, DHS, NIST, and the federal CIO Council worked closely together to develop the United States Government Configuration Baseline (USGCB) for Windows 7 and Internet Explorer 8. As a baseline, USGCB is the core set of default security configurations for all agencies; however, agencies may customize the USGCB baseline to fit their operational needs. In fiscal year 2011, the USGCB was expanded to include RedHat Enterprise Linux 5 Desktop, and multiple updates for Windows 7 and Internet Explorer 8 were released.

Although guidance for implementing appropriate cybersecurity controls has been available for many years, we have consistently identified weaknesses in agencies' implementation of the guidance in control areas such as configuration management. Configuration management is an important process for establishing and maintaining secure information system configurations, and provides important support for managing security risks in information systems. However, inspectors general have consistently reported weaknesses in agencies' implementation of such controls. For example, the fiscal year 2011 report to Congress on the implementation of FISMA listed configuration management as one of the 11 cybersecurity program areas[50] that needed the most improvement. According to that report, 18 of 24 agencies' configuration management programs needed significant improvement. The following deficiencies were found to be the most common:

- configuration management policy was not fully developed (13 of 23 agencies),
- configuration management procedures were not fully developed (9 of 23 agencies),
- standard baseline configurations were not identified for all hardware components (9 of 23 agencies), and
- USGCB was not fully implemented (8 of 23 agencies).

Our own analysis of weaknesses reported by agency inspectors general also shows that the number of weaknesses related to configuration management has increased over the last 4 years. In fiscal year 2008, inspectors general from 15 agencies reported weaknesses related to configuration management, whereas 23 reported weaknesses in 2011.

The experts we consulted focused on the need for security controls to be included in systems development, instead of being applied as an afterthought. One expert stated that commercial companies often forgo the extra cost associated with meeting defined cybersecurity specifications, and security is weakened as a result of the lack of built-in controls. Another expert made a similar comment by saying that one of the most significant changes that would improve cybersecurity is building in security instead of "bolting it on" after the fact. He added that this would involve changing the mindset of various stakeholders.

Monitoring Results

According to NIST, security control effectiveness is measured by correctness of implementation and by how adequately the implemented controls meet organizational needs in accordance with current risk tolerance (i.e., whether the control is implemented in accordance with the security plan to address threats and whether the security plan is adequate). Further, according to NIST, a key element in implementing an effective risk management approach is to establish a continuous monitoring program. Continuous monitoring is the process of maintaining an ongoing awareness of information security, vulnerabilities, and threats to support organizational risk management decisions. The objectives are to (1) conduct ongoing monitoring of the security of an organization's networks, information, and systems; and (2) respond by accepting, transferring, or mitigating risk as situations change. Continuous monitoring is one of the six steps in NIST's risk management framework and is an important way to assess the security impacts on an information system due to changes in hardware, software, firmware, or environmental operations. As part of its reporting instructions since fiscal year 2010, OMB requested inspectors general to report whether agencies had established continuous monitoring programs. For fiscal year 2011, the administration identified continuous monitoring as one of three FISMA priorities, and therefore the fiscal year 2011 FISMA reporting instructions included expanded metrics related to continuous monitoring.

OMB's fiscal year 2011 report on the implementation of FISMA shows that, according to agency reporting, implementation of automated continuous monitoring capabilities rose from 56 percent of total assets in fiscal year 2010 to 78 percent of total assets in fiscal year 2011. Agencies reported that they had implemented automated capabilities for activities such as inventorying assets, configuration management, and vulnerability management, which contributed to improvements in continuous monitoring capabilities (see figure 5).

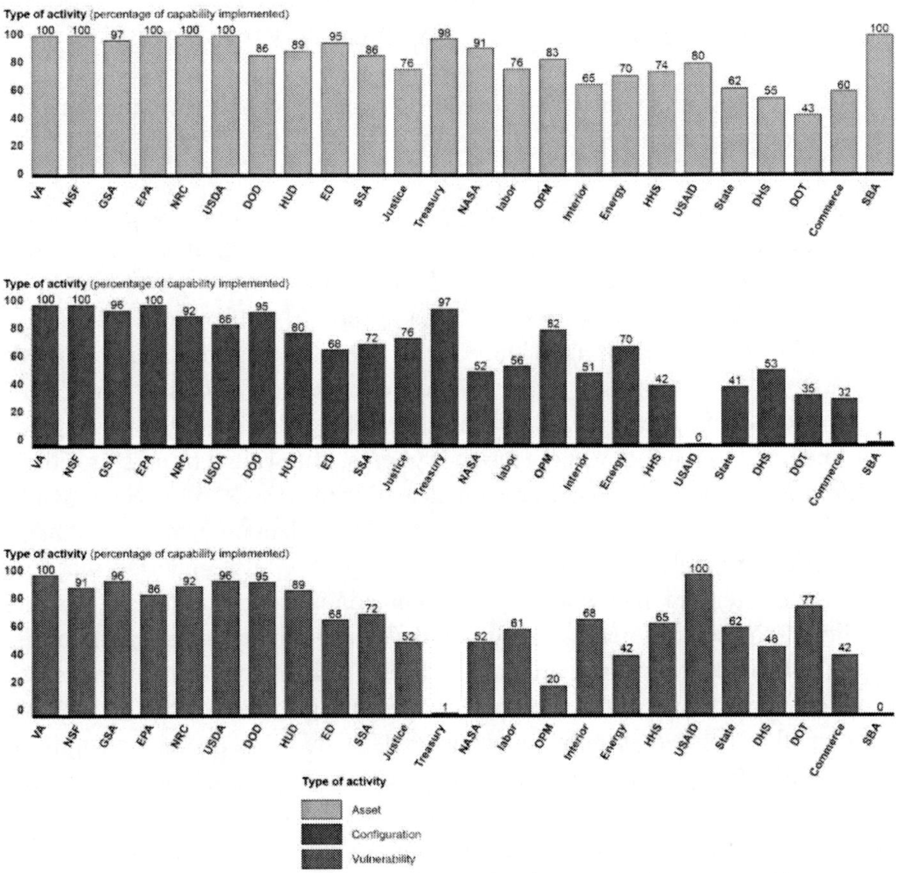

Source: Office of Management and Budget's Fiscal Year 2011 Report to Congress on the Implementation of The Federal Information Management Act of 2002.

Figure 5. Percentage of Continuous Monitoring Capabilities Reported by Agencies in Fiscal Year 2011.

However, the report also states that inspectors general cited 4 out of 11 cybersecurity program areas, including continuous monitoring, as needing the most improvement. The weaknesses in continuous monitoring management most reported by agency inspectors general were

- continuous monitoring policy was not fully developed (9 of 23 agencies),
- key security documentation was not provided to the system authorizing official or other key system officials (8 of 23 agencies), and
- continuous monitoring procedures were not consistently implemented (7 of 23 agencies).

Similarly, in October 2011, we reported that most of the 24 major federal agencies had not fully implemented their programs for continuous monitoring of security controls in fiscal year 2010.[51] We and inspectors general identified weaknesses in 17 of 24 agencies' fiscal year 2010 efforts for continuous monitoring. In addition, in a July 2011 report we stated that while the Department of State is recognized as a leader in federal efforts to develop and implement a continuous risk monitoring capability, this capability's scope did not include non-Windows operating systems, firewalls, routers, switches, mainframes, databases, and intrusion detection devices.[52] We recommended that State take several steps to improve the implementation of its continuous monitoring capability. Further, 2 inspectors general also reported that their respective agencies had not established a continuous monitoring program. While 15 inspectors general reported that their agencies had programs in place, all cited weaknesses in their agencies' programs. These weaknesses included, for example, that continuous monitoring procedures were not fully developed or consistently implemented at 11 agencies. In another example, 10 inspectors general cited weaknesses in ongoing assessments of selected security controls.

Experts had mixed views about the importance of continuous monitoring as a tool to improve cybersecurity in the federal government. While one of the experts we consulted stated that moving from a paperwork-intensive process to a continuous monitoring process was the single most important action that could be taken to improve federal information security, another expert cited penetration testing as the single most important action. Two of the CIOs we surveyed also stated that the move to relying on automated tools to continuously monitor government systems is a practical way to contribute to meaningful security.

Although federal agencies are making progress in implementing continuous monitoring programs that include automated capabilities for managing agency assets, configuration management, and vulnerability management, much more progress is needed to meet the administration's goal for continuous monitoring. Until agencies can fully implement their continuous monitoring programs, they may have little assurance that they are aware of the true security impacts on their information and information systems due to changes in hardware, software, firmware, or environmental operations.

Given the persistent shortcomings in all three key elements of agency risk management processes—assessment, implementation of controls, and monitoring results—it is important that a clearly defined OMB oversight process be in place to ensure that agencies are held accountable for implementing required risk management processes. Without a means to hold agencies accountable, the pattern of persistent risk management shortcomings is unlikely to improve.

GAO Has Previously Reported on Challenges in Coordinating Critical Infrastructure Sector Efforts

DHS and sector-specific agencies have responsibilities for facilitating the adoption of cybersecurity protective measures within critical infrastructure sectors. The NIPP states that, in accordance with HSPD-7, DHS is a principal focal point for the security of cyberspace and is responsible for coordinating efforts to protect the cyber infrastructure owned and operated by the private sector and is responsible for providing guidance on effective cyber-protective measures, assisting sector-specific agencies in understanding and mitigating cyber risk, and assisting in developing effective and appropriate protective measures. To accomplish these responsibilities, according to the NIPP, sector-specific agencies are to work with their private sector counterparts to understand and mitigate cyber risk by, among other things, determining whether approaches for critical infrastructure inventory, risk assessment, and protective measures address assets, systems, and networks; require enhancement; or require the use of alternative approaches.

Security controls for critical infrastructure are likely to be determined largely by industry benchmarks and standards. In some instances, federal agencies have regulatory authority to require private sector implementation of controls. Some controls have also been recommended by federal agencies. In other areas there is little or no federal regulation of private sector cybersecurity practices. For example, as we reported in December 2011, the information technology, communications, and water critical infrastructure sectors and the oil and natural gas subsector of the energy sector are not subject to direct federal cybersecurity-related regulation.[53]

Our December 2011 report stated that although the use of cybersecurity guidance is not mandatory for all sectors, entities may voluntarily implement such guidance in response to business incentives, including the need to mitigate a variety of risks. Officials familiar with cybersecurity issues from both the communications and information technology sectors stated that the competitive market place, desire to maintain profits, and customer expectation of information security—rather than federal regulation—drive the adoption of best practices. Officials responsible for coordinating the oil and gas sector said that their member companies are not required to follow industry guidelines, but legal repercussions regarding standards of care may motivate the incorporation of such cybersecurity guidance into their operations.

Other critical infrastructure entities, such as depository institutions in the banking and finance sector; the bulk power system in the electricity subsector of the energy sector; the health care and public health sector; and the nuclear reactors, materials, and waste sector, are required to meet mandatory cybersecurity standards established by federal regulation. For example, the Federal Energy Regulatory Commission approved eight mandatory cybersecurity standards that address the following topics: critical cyber asset identification, security management controls, personnel and training, electronic security perimeter(s),[54] physical security of critical cyber assets, systems security management, incident reporting and response planning, and recovery plans for critical cyber assets. However, applicability of these standards is limited to the bulk power system—a term that refers to facilities and control systems necessary for operating the electric transmission network and certain generation facilities needed for reliability. Further, regulatory oversight of the electric industry is fragmented among federal, state, and local authorities, thus posing challenges in gaining a system-wide view of the cyber risk to the electric grid in an environment where cyber threats and vulnerabilities of one segment of the grid could affect the entire grid.

DHS's Office of Cybersecurity and Communications' Control Systems Security Program has also issued recommended practices to reduce risks to industrial control systems within and across all critical infrastructure sectors. For example, in April 2011, the program issued the *Catalog of Control Systems Security: Recommendations for Standards Developers*, which is intended to provide a detailed listing of recommended controls from several standards related to control systems.[55] Individual industries and critical infrastructure sectors also have their own specific standards, and some are required to comply with regulations that include cybersecurity. These include standards or guidance developed by regulatory agencies that assist entities within sectors in complying with cybersecurity-related laws and regulations.

However, at the time of our report, DHS and the other sector-specific agencies had not yet identified cybersecurity guidance applicable to or widely used in each of the critical infrastructure sectors. Specifically, DHS guidance for preparing the sector-specific critical infrastructure protection plans called for, among other things, outlining each sector's cyber protection and resilience strategies; however, these plans largely did not identify key guidance for cybersecurity. Only one of the seven sectors we reviewed (banking and finance) listed cybersecurity guidance in its sector- specific plan. We recommended that DHS, in collaboration with the sector-specific agencies, sector coordinating councils, and the owners and operators of cyber-reliant critical infrastructure for the associated seven critical infrastructure sectors, determine whether it is appropriate to have key cybersecurity guidance listed in sector plans or annual plans and adjust planning guidance accordingly to suggest the inclusion of such guidance in future plans. The agency concurred with our recommendation.

Many of the experts we consulted agreed that private sector companies controlling critical infrastructure had not done enough to protect against cyber threats and that the government had not done enough to engage these companies in efforts to enhance cybersecurity. Experts told us that the limited commitment of private sector companies to implement the government's cybersecurity strategy was due to the fact that the government had not made a convincing business case, or value proposition, that specific threats affecting these companies merited substantial new investment in enhanced cybersecurity controls.

We continue to believe that DHS, in collaboration with key private sector entities, should implement our recommendation to determine whether it is appropriate to have key cybersecurity guidance listed in sector plans or annual plans and adjust planning guidance accordingly to suggest the inclusion of such guidance in future plans.

Information Sharing and Timely Analysis and Warning Challenge Federal Efforts to Detect, Respond to, and Mitigate Cybersecurity Incidents

FISMA recognizes incident response as a key element in safeguarding agencies' information systems, and assisting in enhanced security and risk management. The White House and DHS have issued strategies for identifying and responding to cyber incidents affecting both federal information systems and the nation's critical infrastructure and emphasize sharing information, developing analysis and warning capabilities, and coordinating efforts. However, despite efforts made to improve the coordination of information sharing and development of a timely analysis and warning capability, agency officials and experts we consulted confirmed that these areas remain challenges.

Government Strategies for Identifying and Responding to Cybersecurity Incidents Have Emphasized Information Sharing, Analysis and Warning Capabilities, and Coordination

Since 2000, government strategies have identified the need to improve incident response, detection, and mitigation both within the federal government and across the nation. These strategies have consistently emphasized the importance of information sharing, analysis and warning capabilities, and coordinating efforts among relevant entities to minimize the impact of incidents.

The 2000 *National Plan for Information Systems Protection* was largely focused on preparing for and responding to cyber incidents. Two of its three overall objectives were to:

- Prepare for and prevent cyber attacks. This objective was aimed at minimizing the possibility of a significant attack and building an infrastructure that would remain effective in the face of such an attack.
- Detect and respond to cyber attacks. This objective focused on identifying and assessing attacks in a timely way, containing the attacks, and quickly recovering from them.

The plan established programmatic elements and specific activities to achieve each objective with target completion dates. For example, programmatic elements to meet the "detect and respond" objective included detecting unauthorized intrusions, creating incident response capabilities, and sharing attack warnings in a timely manner. Specific activities to address these programmatic elements included developing a pilot intrusion detection network for civilian federal agencies and mechanisms for the regular sharing of federal threat, vulnerability, and warning data with private sector Information Sharing and Analysis Centers (ISAC).[56]

The 2003 *National Strategy to Secure Cyberspace* assigned DHS the lead responsibility for coordinating incident response and recovery planning as well as conducting incident response exercises. The strategy set three objectives that mirror those of the 2000 plan:

- prevent cyber attacks against America's critical infrastructures,
- reduce national vulnerability to cyber attacks, and
- minimize damage and recovery time from cyber attacks that do occur.

Developing a national cybersecurity response system was identified as one of five national priorities, and activities were identified to achieve this priority. According to the strategy, an effective national cyberspace response system would involve public and private institutions and cyber centers performing analysis, conducting watch and warning activities, enabling information exchange, and facilitating restoration efforts. The strategy recommended, among other things, that DHS create a single point of contact for the federal government's interaction with industry and other partners, which would include cyberspace analysis, warning, information sharing, incident response, and national-level recovery efforts. In response to the strategy's recommendations, DHS established US-CERT, which is charged with defending against and helping to respond to cyber attacks on executive branch agencies as well as sharing information and collaborating with state and local governments, industry, and international partners.

The 2003 strategy also stated that DHS would use exercises to evaluate the impact of cyber attacks on government-wide processes. Such exercises were to include critical infrastructure that could have an impact on government-wide processes. According to DHS, it has conducted several exercises since the strategy was issued, including four national- level exercises through its National Exercise program[57] and four Cyber Storm[58] exercises under DHS's Office of Cybersecurity and Communications.

The 2008 CNCI included several projects designed to limit the government's susceptibility to attack and improve its ability to detect and respond to cyber incidents. Unlike the previous strategies, the CNCI focused on technical solutions for incident detection and response. The CNCI projects included the trusted Internet connections initiative, which aimed to limit the ways in which attackers could gain access to federal networks by consolidating external access points, and phases 2 and 3 of the National Cybersecurity Protection System (operationally known as EINSTEIN).[59] The EINSTEIN 2 project involved deploying sensors to inspect Internet traffic entering federal systems for unauthorized accesses and malicious content. EINSTEIN 3's goal was to identify and characterize malicious network traffic to enhance cybersecurity analysis, situational awareness, and security response.

The NIPP sets out a strategy for strengthening national preparedness, timely response, and rapid recovery of critical infrastructure from cyber attacks or other emergencies. According to the NIPP, this goal can be achieved by building partnerships with federal agencies; state, local, tribal, and territorial governments; the private sector; international entities; and non-governmental organizations to share information and implement critical infrastructure protection programs and resilience strategies. Accordingly, the NIPP relies on public-private partnerships to coordinate information-sharing activities related to cybersecurity. It also encourages private sector involvement by establishing sector coordinating councils for each critical infrastructure sector established by HSPD-7. Sectors also utilize ISACs, which provide operational and tactical capabilities for information sharing and, in some cases, support for incident response activities. Through the public-private partnership, the government and private sectors are to work in tandem to create the context, framework, and support for coordination and information-sharing activities required to implement and sustain a specific sector's critical infrastructure protection efforts. The NIPP also states that government and private sector partners are to work together to ensure that exercises include adequate testing of critical infrastructure protection measures and plans, including information sharing.

The 2009 *Cyberspace Policy Review* subsequently concluded that previous federal responses to cyber incidents were less than fully effective because they had not been fully integrated, thus returning to an emphasis on information sharing and coordination. For example, it stated that while federal cybersecurity centers often shared their information, no single entity combined all information available from these centers and other sources to provide a continuously updated and comprehensive picture of cyber threats and network activity. Such a comprehensive picture could provide indications and warning of incoming incidents and support a coordinated incident response. The policy review observed that the government needed a reliable and consistent mechanism for bringing all appropriate incident and vulnerability information together and recommended the development of an information-sharing and incident response framework. The review recommended that the federal government leverage existing resources such as the Multi-State Information Sharing and Analysis Center and the 58 state and local fusion centers[60] to develop processes to assist in preventing, detecting, and responding to cyber incidents. Implementation of the recommended framework would require developing reporting thresholds, adaptable response and recovery plans, information sharing, and incident reporting mechanisms.

The review also identified and recommended near and midterm actions, which included preparing a cybersecurity incident response plan, initiating a dialogue to enhance public-private partnerships, and developing a process between the government and the private sector to assist in preventing, detecting, and responding to incidents. In response to the policy review recommendations, DHS drafted the *Interim National Cyber Incident Response Plan* in 2010, which establishes an incident response framework and designates the National Cybersecurity Communications and Integration Center (NCCIC) as the national point of execution for response activities within the scope of DHS authorities. The NCCIC is the point of integration for sharing information from federal agencies, state, local, tribal, and territorial governments, and the private sector, including international stakeholders. According to the response plan, all stakeholders—public and private sector stakeholders, law enforcement agencies, and the intelligence community—are responsible for assessing lessons learned from previous incidents and exercises and incorporating these lessons into their preparedness activities and plans. In addition, organizations are responsible for engaging with the NCCIC, operational organizations like ISACs, and other organizations within the cyber incident response community, among other things, to coordinate incident response activities.

The U.S. Government Faces Challenges in Developing an Incident Response Framework

Despite repeated emphasis on information sharing, analysis and warning capabilities, and coordination, the federal government continues to face challenges in effectively sharing threat and incident information with the private sector and in developing a timely analysis and warning capability. While DHS has made incremental progress in improving its information sharing and developing timely analysis and warning capabilities, these challenges remain.

Information Sharing

According to the 2009 *Cyberspace Policy Review*, sharing of information among entities is key to preventing, detecting, and responding to incidents. Network hardware and software providers, network operators, data owners, security service providers, and in some cases, law enforcement or intelligence organizations may each have information that can contribute to the detection and understanding of sophisticated intrusions or attacks. A full understanding and effective response may only be possible by bringing together information from those various sources for the benefit of all.

DHS has taken steps to facilitate information sharing. For example, in 2010, the DHS inspector general reported that US-CERT had established the Joint Agency Cyber Knowledge Exchange (JACKE)[61] and Government Forum of Incident Response and Security Teams[62] to facilitate collaboration on detecting and mitigating threats to the .gov domain and to encourage proactive and preventative security practices.[63] Additionally, in 2010, the DHS inspector general reported that DHS shared cyber incident information through its Government Forum of Incident Response and Security Teams and US-CERT portals.[64]

In 2008 and 2010, we reported that one of the barriers to information sharing was the lack of individuals with appropriate security clearances to receive classified information related to potential or actual cyber-related incidents, which prevented federal agencies and private sector companies from acting on these incidents in a timely manner.[65] In 2010, we also reported that private sector companies were often unwilling to share incident data because they were concerned about their proprietary data being seen by competitors. We recommended that the Cybersecurity Coordinator and the Secretary of Homeland Security focus their information-sharing efforts on the most desired services, including providing security clearances. Since these reports, DHS stated that it has taken steps to increase the number of individuals in the public and private sector who are granted security clearances and are able to receive classified information related to cyber incidents. According to the DHS inspector general, the department has also coordinated the installation of classified and unclassified information technology systems at fusion centers to support information sharing.[66] In addition, DHS stated that it has established information-sharing agreements between the federal government and the private sector or ISAC, and a program to address private sector partners' concerns related to protecting their proprietary data. Further, DHS reported that, as of May 2012, there were 16 organizations, including federal agencies and private sector companies, operating and participating within the NCCIC to share information. Finally, according to DHS officials, the NCCIC and its components are also collaborating with industry to develop a set of technical specifications intended to help automate information sharing by establishing a framework for exchanging data.

To improve government and critical infrastructure collaboration and public-private cybersecurity data sharing, DHS reported that it had established the Critical Infrastructure Information Sharing and Collaboration Program. The program's goal is to improve sharing among ISACs, information and communications technology service providers, and their respective critical infrastructure owners, operators, and customers. According to DHS, this program facilitated the sharing and distribution of 11,000 indicators of cyber threat activity and over 400 products, including indicator and analysis bulletins. In addition, according to DHS, US-CERT has incorporated a Traffic Light Protocol into its information-sharing products. The Traffic Light Protocol provides a methodology to specify a color on a product to reflect when information should be used and how it may be shared. In addition, according to a DHS official, in October 2012, DHS's Office of Cybersecurity and Communications was realigned to include all entities reporting to the NCCIC division. This new structure brought all of the department's operational communications and cybersecurity programs together under a single point of coordination.

DHS has not always been able to take action to improve information sharing, however. For example, the Office of the Director of National Intelligence issued a directive on sharing "tear-line" information among intelligence community members, and state, local, tribal, and private sector partners.[67] This policy directs the intelligence community to improve tear-line utility for the needs of recipients prior to publication and specifies that tear lines should be extended to the broadest possible readership. However, DHS does not have the authority to declassify information it receives from other entities. For example, the inspector general reported that DHS cannot generate tear-line reports or release any information that may hinder another agency's ongoing investigation, work in progress, or violate applicable classification policies.[68] Thus DHS was not able to act on the new directive.

Difficulties in sharing and accessing classified information and the lack of a centralized information-sharing system continue to hinder DHS's progress in sharing cyber-related incident data in a timely manner. For example, in December 2011, the DHS inspector general reported that classification of information impedes effective information sharing between officials within fusion centers and emergency operations centers.[69] The inspector general recommended that DHS effectively disseminate and implement a directive to improve policies for safeguarding and governing access to classified information shared by the federal government with state, local, tribal, and private sector entities. DHS concurred with the recommendation. In addition, in July 2012, the DHS former inspector general reported that state and local fusion center personnel had expressed concern with federal information-sharing systems due to the fact that the systems were not integrated and information could not easily be shared across the systems, resulting in continued communication and information-sharing challenges.[70] The DHS inspector general also reported that US-CERT collected and posted information from several systems and sources to different portals, all of which had different classification levels resulting in communication and information-sharing issues.[71] The inspector general recommended that the department establish a consolidated, multiple-classification-level portal that can be accessed by the federal partners and includes real-time incident response related information and reports. According to DHS officials, a secure environment for sharing cybersecurity information, at all classification levels, intended to address these issues is scheduled to be fully operational in fiscal year 2018.

Information sharing presents a challenge not only within the nation, but also with the international community. In August 2012, the DHS inspector general reported that information sharing with foreign partners has been hindered due, in part, to varying classification policies.[72] Foreign governments have developed their own policies for classifying sensitive information, which has resulted in inconsistencies in classifying information among different countries. According to the inspector general, an international team surveyed indicated that inconsistent classification requirements hinder foreign countries' abilities to share cyber threat data in a timely manner, as information shared must be approved by different authorities in various countries before it can be disseminated to international partners and private organizations. The inspector general recommended that DHS conduct information-sharing assessments to identify internal gaps and impediments in order to increase situational awareness and enhance collaboration with foreign nations. DHS concurred with the recommendation.

Agency officials, CIOs, and experts we consulted agreed that information sharing remains a significant challenge. According to a DHS official, despite the NCCIC being in operation, there are still challenges with coordinating and sharing information. The official explained that these challenges are due in part to DHS's lack of authority over agencies' information-sharing practices and the private sector's cybersecurity efforts, and that agencies and private sector companies are not always able to identify the benefit of reporting information to DHS. Seven out of the 11 CIOs that responded to our survey stated that the most effective way to enhance information sharing would be to develop a streamlined process for declassifying key information and making it available to stakeholders. One CIO also explained that the current process for notifying agencies about incidents lacks specificity, making it unclear what the threat is and how to mitigate it. The CIO added that a declassification process would be helpful. Several CIOs stated the most effective way to enhance information sharing would be to improve the timeliness of incident information reports. Further, 6 of the 11 CIOs indicated that focused information-sharing efforts, including working toward increased private sector engagement and a robust information-sharing framework, are the most important actions that the federal government can take now to improve protection of cyber critical infrastructure. Six CIOs also stated that improving information sharing and coordination is the most important action that the federal government could take to improve the national response to large-scale cyber events.

Several experts surveyed agreed that information sharing is a challenge. For example, one expert stated that the most important action that can be taken now to improve federal information security is improving information sharing. The expert explained that real-time information sharing between different branches of government, including the Department of Defense and intelligence community, would be valuable. In addition, experts stated that information sharing is one of the most significant challenges in improving the nation's cybersecurity posture.

Developing a Timely Analysis and Warning Capability

Establishing analytical and warning capabilities is essential to thwarting cyber threats and attacks. Cyber analysis and warning capabilities include (1) monitoring network activity to detect anomalies, (2) analyzing information and investigating anomalies to determine whether they are threats, (3) warning appropriate officials with timely and actionable threat and mitigation information, and (4) responding to threats. The 2009 *Cyberspace Policy Review* identified a need for the federal government to improve its ability to provide strategic warning of cyber intrusions. In 2008, we identified 15 key attributes associated with these capabilities, including integrating the results of the analysis of the information into predictive analysis of broader implications or potential future attacks.[73] This type of effort—predictive analysis—should look beyond one specific incident to consider a broader set of incidents or implications that may indicate a potential threat of importance.

US-CERT has established a cyber analysis and warning capability that includes many elements of the key attributes we identified in our 2008 report. For example, it obtains internal network operation information via technical tools and EINSTEIN; obtains external information on threats, vulnerabilities, and incidents; and detects anomalous activities based on the information it receives. To help improve the federal government's analysis and warning capability, DHS has completed several actions. For example, according to DHS, the department has (1) increased its cybersecurity workforce, (2) improved the training available to federal staff, such as periodic training on EINSTEIN capabilities; and (3) launched a loaned executive program to obtain ad hoc, unpaid, short- term expertise through appointment of private sector individuals.

According to DHS, to strengthen its analytical capabilities, it is using an analysis tool to enhance its ability to track malicious activity. DHS also reported utilizing a cyber indicators analysis platform that acts as a centralized repository for cyber threat network data and facilitates information exchange among US-CERT and its partners to conduct analysis. Also, DHS has established the NCCIC as its 24-hour cyber and communications watch and warning center with representation from law enforcement and intelligence organizations, computer emergency response teams, and private sector information-sharing and analysis centers.[74] Furthermore, according to DHS, intrusion detection capabilities have been expanded, and 53 federal agencies are now using EINSTEIN 2 intrusion detection sensors. DHS staff have also stated that the department is incorporating an EINSTEIN 3 accelerated (E^3A) strategy allowing for accelerated deployment of intrusion prevention services through an Internet Service Provider-based managed security service. According to DHS, the E^3A approach represents a shift from DHS's previous partnership with the National Security Agency for implementation of National Security Agency-developed intrusion technology to a partnership between DHS and commercial providers for the utilization of commercial intrusion prevention technologies.

In addition, to improve DHS's understanding of the extent to which the EINSTEIN program is meeting its objective to improve situational awareness of activity across the federal government, DHS developed performance measures to monitor and track agency responses to EINSTEIN alerts. For example, according to DHS, it tracks: (1) when an agency responds to an alert,

(2) total hours taken by an agency in response to an alert, and (3) length of time of each alert.

Despite these efforts, establishing a timely analysis and warning capability remains a challenge. In 2008, we reported that DHS lacked a predictive analysis capability and had not yet defined methodologies and indicators.[75] We recommended that the Secretary of Homeland Security expand capabilities to investigate incidents. In response to our report, DHS stated that while it has made progress in developing its predictive capability through the EINSTEIN program, it remained challenged in fully developing this capability. DHS plans to test tools for predictive analysis across federal agencies and private networks and systems by the first quarter of fiscal year 2013. In addition, in 2010, the DHS inspector general reported that the tools US-CERT used did not allow for real-time analyses of network traffic.[76] The inspector general recommended that DHS establish a capability to share real-time EINSTEIN information with federal agency partners to assist them in the analysis and mitigation of incidents. In response to the inspector general report, DHS stated that while it plans to upgrade its capabilities to share real-time information with multiple stakeholders and better analyze cyber incidents, these capabilities are not expected to be fully operational until fiscal year 2018.

In addition, agency CIOs and experts that responded to our survey indicated that developing a timely analysis and warning capability remains a challenge due in part to personnel changes, a lack of qualified personnel and incentives, and the lack of appropriate tools. For example, one CIO stated that there has been a significant amount of turnover of cyber leadership at DHS and that this is one of the most significant challenges to improving the nation's cybersecurity posture. Another CIO indicated that increased funding, hiring of more qualified personnel, and more timely notifications would also significantly assist in developing timely warning capabilities. Likewise, a cybersecurity expert we interviewed agreed that DHS may be losing skilled personnel to the private sector because of incentives such as higher salaries. A federal CIO further stated that additional funding was needed for monitoring and intrusion prevention tools.

DHS has taken a number of steps to improve information sharing and timely analysis and warning capabilities, including addressing many of our prior recommendations. However, it has not yet fully addressed all of the recommendations made by us and the inspector general. We continue to believe that DHS needs to fully implement these recommendations in order to make better progress in addressing the challenges associated with effectively responding to and mitigating cybersecurity incidents. Until the previous recommendations are addressed, these challenges are likely to persist.

Addressing Challenges in Promoting Education, Increasing Awareness, and Workforce Planning Is Key to Implementing a Successful Cybersecurity Strategy

NIST includes education as a key element in its guidance to agencies, noting that establishing and maintaining a robust and relevant information-security training and awareness program is the primary conduit for providing the workforce with the information and tools needed to protect an agency's vital information resources. Specifically, the ability to secure federal systems is dependent on the knowledge, skills, and abilities of the federal and contractor workforce that uses, implements, secures, and maintains these systems. This includes federal and contractor employees who use IT systems in the course of their work as well as the designers, developers, programmers, and administrators of the programs and systems.

Workforce planning addresses education at a strategic, agency-wide level. Our own work[77] and the work of other organizations, such as the Office of Personnel Management (OPM),[78] suggest that there are leading practices that workforce planning should address, including

- developing workforce plans that link to the agency's strategic plan;
- identifying the type and number of staff needed for an agency to achieve its mission and goals;
- defining roles, responsibilities, skills, and competencies for key positions;
- developing strategies to address recruiting needs and barriers to filing cybersecurity positions;
- ensuring compensation incentives and flexibilities are effectively used to recruit and retain employees for key positions;
- ensuring compensation systems are designed to help the agency compete for and retain the talent it needs to attain its goals; and
- establishing a training and development program that supports the competencies the agency needs to accomplish its mission.

Federal Strategy Documents Have Consistently Included Elements Addressing Education, Awareness, and Workforce Planning

The 2000 *National Plan for Information Systems Protection* stated that a cadre of trained computer science and information technology specialists was the most urgently needed solution for building a defense of our nation's cyberspace, but the hardest to acquire. The plan proposed steps to stimulate the higher education market to produce more cybersecurity professionals. Specifically, the plan described five Federal Cyber Services (now CyberCorps) training and education programs intended to help solve the federal IT security personnel problem. These five programs were an occupational study to assess the numbers and qualifications of IT positions in the federal government, the development of Centers for Information Technology Excellence,[79] the creation of a scholarship program to recruit and educate federal IT personnel, the development of a high school recruitment and training initiative, and the development and implementation of a federal information security awareness curriculum. At the time, these programs were targeted for implementation by May 2002.

The 2003 *National Strategy to Secure Cyberspace* also recognized the importance of education, awareness, and training, expanding the focus of the 2000 plan on building a stronger workforce, to include a national security awareness and training program as one of its five priority areas. The strategy identified four major actions and initiatives to address this priority. They were

- foster adequate training and education programs to support the nation's cybersecurity needs;
- promote a comprehensive national awareness program to empower all Americans—businesses, the general workforce, and the general population—to secure their own parts of cyberspace;
- increase the efficiency of existing federal cybersecurity training programs; and
- promote private-sector support for well-coordinated, widely recognized professional cybersecurity certifications.

The 2003 strategy recommended that DHS be the lead agency responsible for implementing programs to address its four major actions and initiatives. To foster adequate training and education programs, DHS was charged with implementing and encouraging establishment of training programs for cybersecurity professionals in coordination with the National Science Foundation, OPM, and the National Security Agency. DHS was also charged with developing a coordination mechanism for federal cybersecurity and computer forensics training programs and encouraging private sector support for professional cybersecurity certifications. To increase public awareness, DHS was asked to facilitate a comprehensive awareness campaign; encourage and support the development of programs and guidelines for primary and secondary school students in cybersecurity; and create a public-private task force to identify ways to make it easier for home users and small businesses to secure their systems.

The 2008 CNCI focused again on the cybersecurity workforce and included a training program for cybersecurity professionals among its 12 programs. Specifically, CNCI called for constructing a comprehensive federal cyber education and training program, with attention to offensive and defensive skills and capabilities. The CNCI education and training project was assigned to DHS and DOD as a joint effort, altering the responsibilities defined in the 2003 strategy.

The 2009 White House *Cyberspace Policy Review* also noted the importance of cybersecurity education, awareness, and workforce planning. It stated that the United States needed a technologically advanced workforce and that the general public needed to be well informed about how to use technology safely. To do this, it recommended (1) promoting cybersecurity risk awareness for all citizens; (2) building an education system to enhance understanding of cybersecurity and allow the United States to retain and expand upon its scientific, engineering, and market leadership in information technology; (3) expanding and training the workforce to protect the nation's competitive advantage; and (4) helping organizations and individuals make smart choices as they manage risk. It named the Cybersecurity Coordinator as the lead for the development and implementation of a public awareness strategy and a strategy for better attracting cybersecurity expertise and increasing cybersecurity staff retention within the federal government. It tasked all departments and agencies with expanding support for key education programs and facilitating programs and information sharing on threats, vulnerabilities, and effective practices across all levels of government and industry.

Consistent with the federal government's evolving strategy for education, awareness, and workforce planning, DHS, NIST, and other agencies have initiated a comprehensive cybersecurity education program that includes education, awareness, and workforce planning. In April 2010, the National Initiative for Cybersecurity Education (NICE) was begun as an interagency effort coordinated by NIST to improve cybersecurity education, including efforts directed at training, public awareness, and the federal cybersecurity workforce. To meet NICE objectives, efforts were structured into the following four components:

1. **National Cybersecurity Awareness:** This component included public service campaigns to promote cybersecurity and responsible use of the Internet as well as making cybersecurity popular for children. It was also aimed at making cybersecurity a popular educational and career pursuit for older students.
2. **Formal Cybersecurity Education:** Education programs encompassing K-12, higher education, and vocational programs related to cybersecurity were included in this component, which focused on the science, technology, engineering, and math disciplines to provide a pipeline of skilled workers for private sector and government.
3. **Federal Cybersecurity Workforce Structure:** This component addressed personnel management functions, including the definition of cybersecurity jobs in the federal government and the skills and competencies they required. Also included were new strategies to ensure federal agencies attract, recruit, and retain skilled employees to accomplish cybersecurity missions.
4. **Cybersecurity Workforce Training and Professional Development:** Cybersecurity training and professional development for federal government civilian, military, and contractor personnel were included in this component.

GAO Has Previously Reported that Government-wide Education Initiatives Have Made Mixed Progress

In March 2010, we reported that CNCI faced a number of key challenges in achieving its objectives, including reaching agreement among stakeholders on the scope of cybersecurity education efforts.[80] Stakeholders could not reach agreement on whether to address cybersecurity education from a much broader perspective as part of the initiative, or remain focused on the federal cyber workforce. A panel of experts stated at the time that the federal government needed to publicize and raise awareness of the seriousness of the cybersecurity problem and to increase the number of professionals with adequate cybersecurity skills. They went on to say that the cybersecurity discipline should be organized into concrete professional tracks through testing and licensing. Such tracks would increase the federal cybersecurity workforce by strengthening the hiring and retention of cybersecurity professionals. We recommended that the Director of National Intelligence and the OMB Director reach agreement on the scope of CNCI's education projects to ensure that an adequate cadre of skilled personnel was developed to protect federal information systems. The scope of the CNCI education projects was subsequently expanded from a federal focus to a larger national focus.

In August 2011, NIST released a draft version of the NICE Strategic Plan that included the high-level goals and vision for cybersecurity education. In November 2011, we reported that while the NICE strategic plan described several ambitious outcomes, the departments involved in NICE had not developed details on how they were going to achieve the outcomes.[81] We further reported that specific tasks under and responsibilities for NICE activities were unclear and a formal governance structure was missing. We recommended that Commerce, OMB, OPM, and DHS collaborate through the NICE initiative to clarify the governance structure for NICE to specify responsibilities and processes for planning and monitoring of initiative activities; and develop and finalize detailed plans allowing agency accountability, measurement of progress, and determination of resources to accomplish agreed-upon activities. Since then, DHS has developed a plan for its role in implementing NICE. Although the plan does not contain detailed steps on how the department will achieve the stated goals, it does include a timeline for completion and immediate and long-term recommended calls to action. In addition, in support of the NICE initiative, the National Security Agency established a program in April 2012 for the Academic Centers of Excellence in Cyber Operations to further the goal of broadening the pool of skilled cybersecurity workers. This program provides a particular emphasis on technologies and techniques related to specialized cyber operations to enhance the national security posture of the United States.

We have also evaluated the extent to which federal agencies have implemented and established workforce planning practices for cybersecurity personnel. In November 2011, we reported on the progress selected agencies had made in developing workforce plans that specifically define cybersecurity needs.[82] Of the eight agencies we reviewed, only two—DOD and the Department of Transportation (DOT)— had developed workforce plans that addressed cybersecurity. DHS and the Department of Justice had plans that, although not specific to cybersecurity, did address cybersecurity personnel. One agency—the Department of Veterans Affairs (VA)—had a guide on implementing competency models that addressed elements of workforce planning. The remaining three agencies—the Department of Commerce, the

Department of Health and Human Services (HHS), and the Department of the Treasury—had neither departmental workforce plans nor workforce plans that specifically addressed cybersecurity workforce needs. Additionally, data provided from various sources on these agencies' cybersecurity workforce numbers were inconsistent due, in part, to the challenge of defining cybersecurity positions. These agencies had generally taken steps to define cybersecurity roles and responsibilities and related skills and competencies; however, the approaches taken by each agency varied considerably. All eight agencies reported challenges with filling cybersecurity positions. Further, only three of the eight agencies had a department-wide training program for their cybersecurity workforce. Two of the three had established certification requirements for cybersecurity positions.

We recommended that Commerce, HHS, and Treasury develop and implement a department-wide cybersecurity workforce plan or ensure that departmental components are conducting appropriate workforce planning activities; that DOD and DOT update their department-wide cybersecurity workforce plan or ensure that departmental components have plans that appropriately address human capital approaches, critical skills, competencies, and supporting requirements for their cybersecurity workforce strategies; and that VA update its department-wide cybersecurity competency model or establish a cybersecurity workforce plan that fully addresses gaps in human capital approaches and critical skills and competencies, supporting requirements for its cybersecurity workforce strategies, and monitoring and evaluating agency progress. In addition, to help federal agencies better identify their cybersecurity workforce and to improve cybersecurity workforce efforts, we recommended that OPM identify and develop government-wide strategies to address challenges federal agencies face in tracking their cybersecurity workforce; finalize and issue guidance to agencies on how to track the use and effectiveness of incentives for hard-to-fill positions, including cybersecurity positions; and maximize the value of the cybersecurity competency model by (1) developing and implementing a method for ensuring that the competency model accurately reflects the skill set unique to the cybersecurity workforce, (2) developing a method for collecting and tracking data on the use of the competency model, and (3) creating a schedule for revising or updating the model as needed. Five of the agencies concurred with our recommendations, and one agency neither concurred nor nonconcurred with our recommendations.

In August 2012, NIST published the *National Cybersecurity Workforce Framework*, which established a common taxonomy and lexicon that is to be used to describe all cybersecurity work and workers regardless of where or for whom the work is performed. The developers of the framework intended it to be used in the public, private, and academic sectors. According to the framework, the inability to truly understand the cybersecurity workforce will persist, and the nation will be unnecessarily vulnerable to risk, unless the framework is adopted verbatim.

Agency CIOs and Experts Agree Education, Awareness, and Workforce Planning Are a Key Challenge

Of the agency CIOs and experts we surveyed, a substantial number believe education, awareness, and workforce planning are a key challenge. Four of the 11 agency CIOs that responded to our survey, as well as 5 of the 12 experts we surveyed, cited weaknesses in education, awareness, and workforce planning as a root cause hindering progress in improving the nation's cybersecurity posture. According to these CIOs and experts, executives in both federal and private sector organizations often lack a clear understanding of the cybersecurity threat they face and thus often do not make the necessary commitment to developing and maintaining adequate cybersecurity defenses. Specifically, three CIOs stated that the root cause hindering progress in improving the nation's cybersecurity posture is the lack of understanding of the threats and risks to cyber assets. One CIO responded that there does not seem to be sufficient understanding or appreciation of the seriousness of the threats. He went on to state that we must find ways to convince the public that immediate, priority actions are necessary. Two of the cybersecurity experts we surveyed agreed that a poor understanding of the threats and risks was a root cause hindering progress in cybersecurity. For example, one expert stated that it was commonplace for corporate executives to underestimate cybersecurity threats, believing that Internet-based attacks are "not going to happen to me."

In addition, several CIOs and experts were concerned that the cybersecurity workforce was inadequate, both in numbers and training. One CIO stated that role-based qualification standards are needed for the cybersecurity and general workforce with specific actions and activities that are common across the government. He added that the quality of the workforce is one of the largest contributors to the success or failure of a cybersecurity program. During our panel discussion, one expert cited the difficulties in retaining cyber professionals as a challenge. Another panel participant agreed, adding that the lack of cyber professionals at the local government level was also a problem. He added that another challenge was that not enough effort had been spent on implementing planned education and awareness initiatives. For example, he stated that the NICE initiative had stalled in part because funding was devoted to an additional study of the issues involved in education and workforce development.

While DHS and other agencies have taken steps to address our recommendations to clarify the scope of CNCI education initiatives and the governance structure of the NICE initiative, other recommendations have not yet been fully addressed. We continue to believe that OPM and other agencies need to fully implement our recommendations regarding the need to develop and implement department-wide cybersecurity workforce plans or ensure that departmental components are conducting appropriate workforce planning activities. Such actions can contribute to better progress in addressing the challenges associated with enhancing education, awareness, and workforce planning. Until our recommendations are addressed, these challenges are likely to persist.

A National Strategy for Promoting Research and Development Has Not been Fully Implemented

Investing in R&D in cybersecurity technology is essential to creating a broader range of choices and more robust tools for building secure, networked computer systems. The increasing number of incidents and the greater sophistication of cyber threats highlight the importance of investing in R&D to develop new measures to effectively counter these threats. Over the past two decades, federal law and policy have repeatedly called for enhancements to R&D activities to focus on cybersecurity and accelerate useful results.

Federal Laws and Directives Have Promoted Cybersecurity R&D

Several laws and executive directives have called for activities that promote cybersecurity R&D. For example, in 1998, Presidential Decision Directive 63 established a focal point for cybersecurity R&D. It directed OSTP to coordinate research and development agendas and programs for the government through the National Science and Technology Council. The directive stated that R&D should be subject to multiyear planning, take into account private sector research, and be adequately funded to minimize vulnerabilities on a rapid timetable.

In November of 2002, the Cyber Security Research and Development Act authorized funding to the National Institute of Standards and Technology and the National Science Foundation to create more secure cyber technologies and expand cybersecurity R&D. The act called for an increase in federal investment in computer and network security R&D to improve vulnerability assessment, technology, and systems solutions. In addition, it called for an expansion and improved pool of researchers and better coordination of information sharing and collaboration among industry, government, and academic research projects. Also, in 2002, the E-Government Act mandated that OMB ensure the development and maintenance of a government-wide repository of information about federally funded R&D, which would include R&D related to cybersecurity.

HSPD-7, which replaced Presidential Decision Directive 63, also promoted cybersecurity R&D and directed the Department of Commerce to work with private sector, academic, and government organizations to improve technology for cyber systems. It also directed OSTP to coordinate interagency R&D to enhance the protection of critical infrastructure and to assist in preparing an annual federal research and development program.

Federal Strategy Documents Have Also Promoted Cybersecurity Research and Development

In addition to these laws and directives, the federal government has repeatedly adopted cybersecurity strategies that call for enhancing research and development.

For example, in response to Presidential Decision Directive 63, the 2000 *National Plan for Information Systems Protection* called for a critical infrastructure protection R&D program that would rapidly identify, develop, and facilitate technological solutions to existing and emerging infrastructure threats and vulnerabilities. To achieve this goal, the plan recommended that the process include

- an awareness of the state of new technological developments;
- an ability to produce affordable R&D programs in critical infrastructure protection in a timely manner;
- a functioning, effective two-way interaction with the private sector, academia, and other countries to minimize R&D overlap and ensure that the needs of the private sector and government are met; and
- an innovative and flexible management structure that is responsive to rapid changes in the environment in terms of technology and threats.

Additionally, it tasked an interagency working group[83] with ensuring proper coordination of individual R&D programs within and across agencies and the rapid transfer of technologies among agencies and with the private sector. The 2003 *National Strategy to Secure Cyberspace* also noted the importance of R&D. As part of the strategy's priority to reduce threats and related vulnerabilities, it called for the prioritization of federal cybersecurity research and development agendas. To achieve this, the strategy directed OSTP to coordinate development of a federal R&D agenda that included near-term, midterm, and long-term IT security research for fiscal year 2004 and beyond. Like the 2000 plan, it also noted the importance of coordination. The 2003 *National Strategy to Secure Cyberspace* directed DHS to ensure that adequate mechanisms existed for coordination of research and development among academia, industry, and government. DHS was further tasked with facilitating communication between the public and private research and security communities to ensure that emerging technologies were periodically reviewed by the National Science and Technology Council.

The 2008 CNCI included research and development as one of the three overall goals of the initiative and defined specific R&D efforts to achieve those goals. Two of the 12 projects included in the initiative support its R&D goal. Like the 2000 plan and the 2003 strategy, the first project called for OSTP to coordinate and redirect R&D efforts with a focus on better coordinating both classified and unclassified cybersecurity R&D. The second project called for OSTP to define and develop enduring "leap-ahead" technology, strategies, and programs by investing in high-risk, high-reward R&D and by working with both private sector and international partners.

The 2009 *Cyberspace Policy Review* likewise called for the development of a framework for R&D strategies that would focus on "game-changing" technologies with the potential to enhance the security, reliability, resilience, and trustworthiness of digital infrastructure. The policy review asked that the research community be given access to event data to facilitate developing tools, testing theories, and identifying workable solutions. The policy review again focuses on the need for coordination.

According to the review, the government should greatly expand its coordination of R&D work with industry and academic research efforts to avoid duplication, leverage complementary capabilities, and ensure that the technological results of R&D efforts enter the marketplace.

The NIPP also identified R&D as a key element in protecting the nation's critical infrastructure. Like previous strategies, the NIPP identified coordination as a goal for R&D. It stated that federal agencies should work collaboratively to design and execute R&D programs to help develop knowledge and technology to more effectively mitigate the risk to critical infrastructure. The plan described the national critical infrastructure protection R&D plan, which identified three long-term, strategic R&D goals for critical infrastructure protection:

- a "common operating picture" to continuously monitor the health of critical infrastructure;
- a next-generation Internet architecture with designed-in security; and
- resilient, self-diagnosing, self-healing infrastructure systems.

According to the plan, these strategic goals were to be used to guide federal R&D investment decisions and coordinate overall federal research.

As previously stated, in December 2011 OSTP issued the first cybersecurity R&D strategic plan in response to the R&D-related recommendations in the *Cyberspace Policy Review*.[84] According to a key Subcommittee on Networking and Information Technology Research and Development (NITRD)[85] official who works closely with OSTP, the federal cybersecurity R&D strategic plan is intended to provide an overall vision or direction for R&D, while specific research priorities and time frames are to be determined at the agency level.

Poor Coordination Has Hindered Government Support for Cybersecurity R&D

As early as 2000, the *National Plan for Information Systems Protection* acknowledged the challenges of implementing a coordinated R&D program. For example, the plan stated that coordinating federal R&D with ongoing private sector programs would be complicated by industry's desire to guard proprietary programs and trade secrets. Specifically, the plan noted that it was difficult to identify all relevant ongoing R&D programs and that some of them overlapped. In a June 2010 report on research and development, we concluded that despite the continued focus on coordination between federal agencies and the public sector, R&D initiatives were hindered by limited sharing of detailed information about ongoing research.[86] According to federal and private experts we consulted for the 2010 report, key factors existed that reduced the private sector's and government's willingness to share information and trust each other with regard to researching and developing new cybersecurity technologies. Specifically, private sector officials stated that they were often unwilling to share details of their R&D with the government because they wanted to protect their intellectual property. On the government side, officials were concerned that the private sector was too focused on making a profit and may not necessarily conduct R&D in areas that require the most attention.

Additionally, at the time of our report, government and private sector officials indicated that the government did not have a process in place to communicate the results of completed federal R&D projects. The private and public sectors had shared some cybersecurity R&D information, but such information sharing generally occurred only on a project-by-project basis. For example, we reported that the National Science Foundation's Industry University Cooperative Research Center initiative established centers to conduct research that is of interest to both industry and academia, and DOD's Small Business Innovation Research program funded R&D at small technology companies. However, according to federal and private sector experts we consulted at that time, widespread and ongoing information sharing generally had not occurred.

Further, the 2010 report also stated that no complete and up-to-date repository existed to track all cybersecurity R&D information and associated funding as required by law. At that time, an OSTP official indicated that it was difficult to develop and enforce policies for identifying specific funding as R&D, and that the level of detail to be disclosed was also a factor because national security must be protected. To help facilitate information sharing about ongoing and planned R&D projects, we recommended that OSTP, in conjunction with the Cybersecurity Coordinator, direct NITRD to (1) establish a mechanism, consistent with existing law, to keep track of all ongoing and completed federal cybersecurity R&D projects and associated funding; and (2) utilize the newly established tracking mechanism to develop an ongoing process to make federal R&D information available to federal agencies and the private sector. OSTP concurred with our recommendations.

Subsequently, in September 2012, we reported that OMB had not fully established the repository for providing information on R&D funded by the federal government.[87] We found that only 11 of the 24 major agencies in our study reported providing research information to http://www.Science.gov.[88] Moreover, 2 agencies in our study reported not being aware of any R&D repository. OMB officials pointed to an R&D dashboard website being developed by OSTP that was intended to meet the requirement for an R&D repository. However, this website provided information on federal investments in research and development for only 2 agencies.[89] Further, according to OMB, a timeline had not yet been developed for when all agencies were to provide information for the R&D dashboard, and guidance had not been issued for agencies to upload their information to the website.

We continue to believe that implementing our recommendations to OMB to issue guidance on reporting cybersecurity R&D activities and to OSTP to establish a mechanism to track ongoing and completed federal cybersecurity R&D projects is important for addressing challenges associated with effectively promoting cybersecurity R&D in the federal government. Until our recommendations are addressed, these challenges are likely to persist.

The Federal Government Continues to Face International Cybersecurity Challenges

Recent intrusions on U.S. corporations and federal agencies by attackers in foreign countries highlight the threats posed by the worldwide connection of our networks and the need to adequately address the global security and governance of cyberspace. The global interconnectivity provided by the Internet allows cyber attackers to easily cross national borders, access vast numbers of victims at the same time, and easily maintain anonymity. Governance over Internet activities is complicated because Internet users may be able to retrieve or post information or perform an activity which is illegal where they are physically located, but not illegal in the country where the computer they are accessing is located. A number of agencies have responsibilities for, and are involved in, international cyberspace security and governance efforts. Specifically, the Departments of Commerce, Defense, Homeland Security, Justice, and State, among others, are involved in efforts to develop international standards, formulate cyber-defense policy, facilitate overseas investigations and law enforcement, and represent U.S. interests in international forums. Agencies also participate in international organizations and collaborative efforts to influence international cyberspace security and governance, including engaging in bilateral and multilateral relationships with foreign countries, providing personnel to foreign agencies, and coordinating U.S. policy among government agencies.

Strategy Documents Have Included Elements that Address International Coordination

As threats to cyberspace have persisted and grown and cyberspace has expanded globally, the federal government has developed policies, strategies, and initiatives that recognize the importance of addressing cybersecurity on a global basis.

While the 2000 *National Plan for Information Systems Protection* focused on domestic efforts to protect the nation's cyber critical infrastructure, it described U.S. law enforcement collaboration with law enforcement counterparts from other nations to enhance international cooperation and develop a common approach to criminalizing intrusions and attacks on information networks and systems. In addition, the plan noted that national security agencies needed programs regarding permissible roles for national security agency involvement in foreign activities.

The 2003 *National Strategy to Secure Cyberspace* went further by establishing international cyberspace security cooperation as a key part of one of its five national priorities. The strategy stated that securing global cyberspace required international cooperation to raise awareness, share information, promote security standards, and investigate and prosecute cybercrime. The strategy identified five key initiatives, led by the Department of State, to strengthen international cooperation, including

- working through international organizations and with industry to facilitate and promote a global "culture of security";
- developing secure networks;
- promoting North American cyberspace security;
- fostering the establishment of national and international watch-and-warning networks to detect and prevent cyber attacks as they emerge; and
- encouraging other nations to accede to the Council of Europe Convention on Cybercrime, or to ensure that their laws and procedures were at least as comprehensive.

To fulfill the Department of State's lead responsibility, a number of the department's entities were given roles, including having the Bureau of Intelligence and Research, Office of Cyber Affairs, coordinate outreach on cybersecurity issues and the Bureau of International Narcotics and Law Enforcement Affairs coordinate policy and programs to combat cybercrime.

International cooperation is also identified as a priority for critical infrastructure in HSPD-7, which directed DHS to, among other things, develop a strategy for working with international organizations on critical infrastructure protection. The directive also designated State, in conjunction with Commerce, DOD, DHS, Justice, Treasury, and other appropriate agencies, to work with foreign countries and international organizations to strengthen the protection of U.S. critical infrastructure. The requirements set forth in HSPD-7 were addressed with the creation of the NIPP in 2006, and its update in 2009. The NIPP includes a section on international cooperation to protect critical infrastructure that focuses on, among other things, international cybersecurity and cooperation with international partners through activities such as national cyber exercises.

In contrast to the 2003 strategy, the 2008 CNCI did not include international cooperation as one of its 12 component projects. While none of the projects directly addressed international cooperation, one initiative that focused on deterring interference and attacks in cyberspace included a goal of better articulating roles for private sector and international partners. The initiative also recognized the need to develop an approach to better manage the federal government's global supply chain.

The 2009 White House *Cyberspace Policy Review* adhered more closely to the 2003 strategy, identifying international coordination as part of one of its five key topic areas. The review called for the development of an international strategy to foster cooperation on issues such as acceptable legal norms regarding territorial jurisdiction, sovereign responsibility, and the use of force. The review recommended, among other things, that the United States accelerate efforts to help other countries build legal frameworks and capacity to fight cybercrime and continue to promote cybersecurity practices and standards. It also recommended that the Cybersecurity Coordinator work with federal agencies to strengthen and integrate interagency processes to formulate and coordinate international cybersecurity-related positions and to enhance the identification, tracking, and prioritization of international venues, negotiations, and discussions where cybersecurity-related policy-making was taking place. In addition, the review recommended that the federal government work with the private sector to develop a proactive engagement plan for use with international standards bodies, including looking at the policies that already exist and refining them to make sure the full range of cybersecurity interests was taken into account.

DOD and DHS have also identified international coordination as a key aspect of their recently released cyberspace strategies. In July 2011, the *DOD Strategy for Operating in Cyberspace* identified five strategic initiatives, including building relationships with U.S. allies and international partners to strengthen collective cybersecurity. The strategy states that DOD will assist U.S. efforts to develop and promote international cyberspace norms, cooperate with allies to defend U.S. and allied interest in cyberspace, and expand its international cyber cooperation to a wider pool of allied and partner militaries to develop collective self-defense and increase collective deterrence.

The November 2011 DHS *Blueprint for a Secure Cyber Future* makes similar pledges. One of the blueprint's two overarching focus areas—protecting critical information infrastructure—includes international partnerships as a necessary element for success, and many of the capabilities identified within the strategy's four goals for protecting critical information infrastructure are to be developed and implemented in collaboration with international partners. For example, DHS commits to increasing its capacity to deter, investigate, and prosecute crimes committed through the use of cyberspace by, among other things, developing productive international relationships to safeguard and share evidence to bring cyber criminals to justice. DHS also identified multiple capabilities related to information dissemination to international partners in areas such as adverse incidents and proven practices to decrease the spread and impact of hazards.

GAO Has Previously Identified International Cybersecurity Challenges

While progress has been made in identifying the importance of international cooperation and assigning roles and responsibilities related to it, the government's approach for addressing international aspects of cybersecurity has not yet been completely defined and implemented. We have identified significant challenges within the federal government's international cybersecurity efforts. In our March 2010 report focused on the CNCI, we observed that the federal government was facing strategic challenges in areas that are not the subject of existing projects within CNCI but that remained key to achieving the initiative's overall goal of securing federal information systems.[90] One of the strategic challenges we identified was coordinating with international entities. We found that there was no formal strategy for coordinating outreach to international partners for the purposes of standards setting, law enforcement, and information sharing. Accordingly we recommended that the Director of OMB establish a coordinated approach for the federal government in conducting international outreach to address cybersecurity issues strategically.

In July 2010, we reported on additional challenges the government faced regarding international cooperation in addressing global cybersecurity and governance.[91] Specifically, we reported that the government faced a number of challenges that impeded its ability to formulate and implement a coherent approach to addressing the global aspects of cybersecurity, including

- the White House Cybersecurity Coordinator's authority and capacity to effectively coordinate and forge a coherent national approach to cybersecurity, which were needed to lead near-term international goals and objectives from the President's *Cyberspace Policy Review*, were still under development;
- the U.S. government had not documented a clear vision of how the international efforts of federal entities, taken together, supported overarching national goals;
- federal agencies had not demonstrated an ability to coordinate their international activities and project clear policies on a consistent basis;
- some countries had attempted to mandate compliance with their own cybersecurity standards in a manner that risked discriminating against U.S. companies or posed trade barriers to foreign companies that sought to market and sell their products to other countries;
- the federal government lacked a coherent approach toward participating in a broader international framework for responding to cyber incidents with global impact;
- the differences among laws of nations could impede U.S. and foreign efforts to enforce domestic criminal and civil laws related to cyberspace; and
- some federal agencies reported that they participated in efforts that may contribute to developing international norms, but agencies reported challenges such as, that this was a complicated and long-term process and that the absence of agreed-upon definitions for cyberspace-related terminology could impede efforts to develop international norms.

We concluded that until these challenges were addressed, the United States would be at a disadvantage in promoting its national interests in the realm of cyberspace.

Accordingly, we recommended that the Cybersecurity Coordinator, in collaboration with others, take five actions to address these challenges, which included the following:

- Develop with the Departments of Commerce, Defense, Homeland Security, Justice, and State and other relevant federal and nonfederal entities, a comprehensive U.S. global cyberspace strategy that

  - articulates overarching goals, subordinate objectives, specific activities, performance metrics, and reasonable time frames to achieve results;
  - addresses technical standards and policies while taking into consideration U.S. trade; and
  - identifies methods for addressing the enforcement of U.S. civil and criminal law.
- Enhance the interagency coordination mechanisms by ensuring relevant federal entities are engaged and that their efforts, taken together, support U.S. interests in a coherent and consistent fashion.
- Determine, in conjunction with the Departments of Defense and State and other relevant federal entities, which, if any, cyberspace norms should be defined to support U.S. interests in cyberspace and methods for fostering such norms internationally.

Although the White House developed and released the *International Strategy for Cyberspace* in May 2011 that addresses several of our recommendations, it does not include all the elements we recommended. To its credit, the strategy included goals for establishing cyberspace norms that should be accepted internationally and methods for fostering such norms internationally, such as developing cybercrime norms in appropriate forums and incorporating existing efforts. However, the strategy does not fully specify outcome-oriented performance metrics, or time frames for completing activities. For example, the strategy discusses multiple goals and objectives, but does not provide performance metrics to help ensure accountability and gauge results.

We continue to believe that the international strategy should specify outcome-oriented performance metrics, and time frames for completing activities. Including outcome-oriented performance metrics and time frames for completion would help to ensure that agencies with international responsibilities are taking appropriate actions to implement the strategy and are making progress in improving international cooperation. Until our recommendations are addressed, challenges in defining and implementing an approach for addressing international aspects of cybersecurity are likely to persist.

CONCLUSION

Given the range and sophistication of the threats and potential exploits that confront government agencies and the nation's cyber critical infrastructure, it is critical that the government adopt a comprehensive strategic approach to mitigating the risks of successful cybersecurity attacks. Such an approach would not only define priority problem areas but also set a roadmap for allocating and managing appropriate resources, making a convincing business case to justify expenses, identifying organizations' roles and responsibilities, linking goals and priorities, and holding participants accountable for achieving results. However, the federal government's efforts at defining a strategy for cybersecurity have often not fully addressed these key elements, lacking, for example, milestones and performance measures, identified costs and sources of funding, and specific roles and responsibilities. As a result, the government's cybersecurity strategy remains poorly articulated and incomplete. In fact, no integrated, overarching strategy exists that articulates priority actions, assigns responsibilities for performing them, and sets time frames for their completion. In the absence of an integrated strategy, the documents that comprise the government's current strategic approach are of limited value as a tool for mobilizing actions to mitigate the most serious threats facing the nation.

Previous GAO and inspector general reviews as well as federal CIOs and experts have made recommendations to address challenges faced by federal agencies and the private sector in effectively implementing a comprehensive approach to cybersecurity and reducing the risk of successful cybersecurity attacks. Many of these recommendations have not yet been fully addressed, leaving much room for more progress in addressing cybersecurity challenges. In many cases, the causes of these challenges are closely related to the key elements that are missing from the government's cybersecurity strategy. For example, the persistence of shortcomings in agency cybersecurity risk management processes indicates that agencies have not been held accountable for effectively implementing such processes and that oversight mechanisms have not been clear. It is just such oversight and accountability that is poorly defined in cybersecurity strategy documents. Clarifying oversight responsibilities is a topic that could be effectively addressed through legislation.

An overarching strategy that better addresses key desirable characteristics could establish an improved framework to implement national cybersecurity policy and ensure that stated goals and priorities are actively pursued by government agencies and better supported by key private sector entities. To be successful such a strategy would include a clearer process for OMB oversight of agency risk management processes and a roadmap for improving the cybersecurity challenge areas where previous concerns have not been fully addressed. The development and implementation of such a strategy would likely lead to significant progress in furthering strategic goals and lessening persistent weaknesses.

RECOMMENDATIONS FOR EXECUTIVE ACTION

In order to institute a more effective framework for implementing cybersecurity activities, and to help ensure such activities will lead to progress in cybersecurity, we recommend that the White House Cybersecurity Coordinator in the Executive Office of the President develop an overarching federal cybersecurity strategy that includes all key elements of the desirable characteristics of a national strategy, including

- milestones and performance measures for major activities to address stated priorities;
- cost, sources, and justification for needed resources to accomplish stated priorities;
- specific roles and responsibilities of federal organizations related to the strategy's stated priorities; and
- guidance, where appropriate, regarding how this strategy relates to priorities, goals, and objectives stated in other national strategy documents.

This strategy should also better ensure that federal departments and agencies are held accountable for making significant improvements in cybersecurity challenge areas, including designing and implementing risk-based programs; detecting, responding to, and mitigating cyber incidents; promoting education, awareness, and workforce planning; promoting R&D; and addressing international cybersecurity challenges. To address these issues, the strategy should (1) clarify how OMB will oversee agency implementation of requirements for effective risk management processes and (2) establish a roadmap for making significant improvements in cybersecurity challenge areas where previous recommendations have not been fully addressed.

Matter for Congressional Consideration

To address ambiguities in roles and responsibilities that have resulted from recent executive branch actions, Congress should consider legislation to better define roles and responsibilities for implementing and overseeing federal information security programs and for protecting the nation's critical cyber assets.

Agency Comments and Our Evaluation

We provided a draft of this report to the Executive Office of the President, OMB, DHS, DOD, and Commerce. We received comments from the General Counsel of OSTP, who provided comments from both the National Security Staff and OSTP in the Executive Office of the President; the Deputy General Counsel of OMB; the Director of the Departmental GAO-OIG Liaison Office at DHS; and the Special Assistant for Cybersecurity in the Office of the Secretary of Defense. The Executive Office of the President and OMB both commented on our draft recommendations, and the Executive Office of the President concurred with our matter for congressional consideration. The audit liaison officer in the Director's Office of the National Institute of Standards and Technology within the Department of Commerce responded that the department did not have any comments. A summary of comments we received follows.

- The General Counsel of OSTP in the Executive Office of the President provided comments via e-mail in which the National Security Staff stated that the administration agrees that more needs to be done to develop a coherent and comprehensive strategy on cybersecurity and noted that a number of strategies and policies had been issued to address specific cybersecurity topics. According to the National Security Staff, remaining flexible and focusing on achieving measurable improvements in cybersecurity would be more beneficial than developing "yet another strategy on top of existing strategies." We agree that flexibility and a focus on achieving measurable improvements in cybersecurity is critically important and that simply preparing another document, if not integrated with previous documents, would not be helpful. The focus of our recommendation is to develop an overarching strategy that integrates the numerous strategy documents, establish milestones and performance measures, and better ensure that federal departments and agencies are held accountable for making significant improvements in cybersecurity challenge areas. We do not believe the current approach accomplishes this. The National Security Staff also agreed with our matter for congressional consideration and that comprehensive cybersecurity legislation that addresses information sharing and baseline standards for critical infrastructure, among other things, is necessary to mitigate the threats posed in cyberspace. The General Counsel also provided technical comments from OSTP, which we have incorporated into the final report as appropriate.

- In comments provided via e-mail, the Deputy General Counsel at OMB responded to our draft recommendation, stating that OMB's responsibility under FISMA is to "oversee" agency implementation of requirements for effective risk management processes. We agree that FISMA gives OMB the responsibility of overseeing agency implementation of cybersecurity risk management requirements and have changed the wording of our recommendation to reflect OMB's role as specified by the act. The Deputy General Counsel also expressed concern about our description of actions OMB took in 2010 with regard to roles and responsibilities under FISMA. According to the Deputy General Counsel, OMB did not delegate or transfer any statutory authorities to DHS. Instead, DHS exercised its own authorities in taking on additional responsibilities. We disagree. FISMA specifies in detail a number of oversight responsibilities that it assigns to OMB. It was several of these specific responsibilities that in 2010 OMB announced DHS would be assuming. Therefore we conclude that OMB transferred these responsibilities to DHS. More importantly, with these responsibilities now divided between the two organizations, it remains unclear how OMB and DHS are to share oversight of individual departments and agencies.
- The Director of the Departmental GAO-OIG Liaison Office at DHS provided written comments that discussed specific actions the department has taken or plans to take to address challenges we identified, such as information sharing, analysis and warning, and expanding the cybersecurity workforce. He added that the department's *Blueprint for a Secure Cyber Future* aligns with the various national strategies we discuss in this report and addresses the

challenge areas we identified. In addition, the audit liaison officer in the Office of the Chief Financial Officer provided technical comments via e-mail, which we have incorporated into the final report as appropriate.

- The Special Assistant for Cybersecurity in the Office of the Secretary of Defense provided general observations about the draft report as well as technical comments via e-mail. For example, the comments indicated that any update to the national cybersecurity strategy should address ways to make cyberspace more defensible. The Special Assistant for Cybersecurity also acknowledged inconsistencies in departmental guidance but said that DOD officials were not confused about their responsibilities and that future updates to the departmental guidance would clarify cyber policy responsibilities. We agree that clarification of DOD organizations' roles and responsibilities would enhance the department's ability to support DHS during significant domestic cyber incidents. In addition, the comments indicated that cybersecurity strategies should be evaluated in terms of to whom the strategy is addressed (i.e., the federal government or the private sector), the rapidity of change in cybersecurity issues, and the environment for which the strategy is written (i.e., federal civilian government, the military, or the private sector). We agree that these are important factors to consider in developing comprehensive cybersecurity strategies and believe our report reflects these factors. We also believe that the issues we identified remain of critical importance in developing and implementing an effective national cybersecurity strategy. Finally, the comments identified actions DOD has taken or is taking to address challenges related to sharing information, promoting education, and promoting R&D.

Gregory C. Wilshusen
Director, Information Security Issues

Dr. Nabajyoti Barkakati
Chief Technologist
Director, Center for Science, Technology, and Engineering

APPENDIX I. OBJECTIVES, SCOPE, AND METHODOLOGY

Our objectives were to (1) determine the extent to which the national cybersecurity strategy includes key desirable characteristics of effective strategies, and (2) identify challenges faced by the federal government in addressing a strategic approach to cybersecurity, including: (a) establishing a management structure to assess cybersecurity risks, developing and implementing appropriate controls, and measuring results; (b) detecting, responding to, and mitigating the effects of attacks on federal civilian and critical infrastructure; (c) enhancing awareness and promoting education; (d) promoting research and development; and (e) developing partnerships to leverage resources internationally.

To determine the extent to which the national cybersecurity strategy includes key desirable characteristics of effective strategies, we assessed the current national cybersecurity strategy and other government-wide strategies[92] against the desirable characteristics of a national strategy. Our assessment determined the extent to which all of the elements of each desirable characteristic were addressed by the strategies. These desirable characteristics were developed by GAO in 2004.[93] At that time, we identified these characteristics by consulting statutory requirements pertaining to certain strategies we reviewed, as well as legislative and executive branch guidance for other national strategies. In addition, we studied the Government Performance and Results Act of 1993 (GPRA), general literature on strategic planning and performance, and guidance from the Office of Management and Budget (OMB) on the President's Management Agenda. We also gathered published recommendations made by national commissions chartered by Congress; past GAO work; and various research organizations that have commented on national strategies.

To determine and assess challenges faced by the federal government in addressing a strategic approach to cybersecurity, we interviewed agency officials with cybersecurity-related responsibilities from agencies with key responsibilities in protecting federal systems and the nation's cyber infrastructure. These agencies were: the Department of Homeland Security (DHS) (including officials from the Office of Cybersecurity and Communications, the National Cybersecurity and Communications Integration Center, the United States Computer Emergency Readiness Team (US-CERT), Office of Program Analysis and Evaluation, Federal Network Security Branch, and the Critical infrastructure Cyber Protection and Awareness Branch); the Department of Defense (DOD) (including officials from the National Security

Agency and the Defense Information Systems Agency); the Executive Office of the President (including officials from OMB, the National Coordination Office, Office of Science and Technology Policy, and the National Security Staff); and the National Institute of Standards and Technology (NIST).

We also obtained the views of private sector cybersecurity and information management experts and federal chief information officers on the key issues and challenges of the current federal strategy for cybersecurity through convening panel discussions and administering surveys. Our first of two panels consisted of information management experts who are members of GAO's Executive Committee for Information Management and Technology and resulted in documenting their identified key issues and challenges. We further surveyed chief information officers from the 24 agencies identified in the Chief Financial Officers Act to determine their key issues and challenges. Eleven of the 24 chief information officers responded to our survey (see app. II). Our second panel and survey involved a selection of private sector cybersecurity experts. To identify private sector cybersecurity experts, we first obtained a universe of experts by reviewing membership and advisor roles for pertinent cybersecurity boards and commissions (e.g., the Information Security and Privacy Advisory Board and the National Academies' Computer Science and Telecommunications Board), key associations that are leading thinkers on cybersecurity (e.g., the Internet Security Alliance), and witnesses from cybersecurity-related congressional hearings. We then made the initial selections by identifying those individuals[94] or organizations[95] that were listed in multiple independent sources.[96] We also selected the last two White House cybersecurity advisors.

Lastly, we reviewed agency inspector general and GAO reports that previously identified challenges related to government-wide cybersecurity strategies and initiatives, and met with staff from the DHS Office of Inspector General to determine the current status of related recommendations in their prior reports. We then assessed progress in overcoming the inspector general- and GAO-identified challenges through interviews with agency officials and reviewing agency documentation and publicly available data.

We performed our work on the initiative of the U.S. Comptroller General to evaluate the federal government's cybersecurity strategies and understand the status of federal cybersecurity efforts to address challenges in establishing a strategic cybersecurity approach.

We conducted this performance audit from April 2012 to February 2013 in accordance with generally accepted government auditing standards. Those standards require that we plan and perform the audit to obtain sufficient, appropriate evidence to provide a reasonable basis for our findings and conclusions based on our audit objectives. We believe that the evidence obtained provides a reasonable basis for our findings and conclusions based on our audit objectives.

APPENDIX II. LIST OF PANEL AND SURVEY PARTICIPANTS

This appendix lists the names and affiliations of the cybersecurity and information management professionals who participated in the cybersecurity expert panel discussion and the Executive Committee for Information Management and Technology panel discussion, as well as the respondents to our surveys of cybersecurity experts and agency CIOs.

Cybersecurity Expert Panel Discussion Attendees

The names and affiliation of the cybersecurity experts, who participated in the panel held September 14, 2012, in Washington D.C., are as follows:

Stewart A. Baker, Partner, Steptoe & Johnson LLP

Steven M. Bellovin, Professor of Computer Science at Columbia University

Dan Chenok, Executive Director, IBM Center for The Business of Government; Chair of NIST's Information Security and Privacy Advisory Board

Larry Clinton, President and CEO, Internet Security Alliance

Tom Gann, Vice President of Government Relations, McAfee

Seymour E. Goodman, Professor of International Affairs and Computing, Sam Nunn School of International Affairs, College of Computing at Georgia Institute of Technology

Susan Landau, Independent Scholar

Herbert Lin, Chief Scientist, Computer Science and Telecommunications Board, National Research Council of the National Academies

Randy V. Sabett, Counsel, ZwillGen LLP

Howard Schmidt, former Cybersecurity Coordinator, Executive Office of the President of the United States; Special Assistant, President of the United States

Executive Committee for Information Management and Technology Panel Discussion Attendees

The names and affiliation of the experts who participated in the panel discussion held September 12, 2012, in Washington D.C., are as follows:

Lynda Applegate, Harvard Business School
Hank Conrad, CounterPoint Corporation
Mary Culnan, Bentley University
John Flynn, Principal, FK&A Inc.
Peter Neumann, SRI International Computer Science Laboratory
Theresa Pardo, Director, Center for Technology in Government, University at Albany, New York
Douglas Robinson, Executive Director, National Association of State Chief Information Officers (NASCIO)
Paul Rummell, Management Consultant
Dugan Petty, State of Oregon and NASCIO
Eugene H. Spafford, CERIAS, Purdue University
Nancy Stewart, Wal-Mart (retired)
Aldona Valicenti, VP Government Markets, CGI
James B. Whittaker, Whittaker Group
John A. Zachman, President, Zachman International

Expert and CIO Survey Participants

Expert Survey Participants

Stewart A. Baker, Partner, Steptoe & Johnson LLP
Steven M. Bellovin, Professor of Computer Science at Columbia University
Scott Borg, Director and Chief Economist, United States Cyber Consequence Unit
Dan Chenok, Executive Director, IBM Center for the Business of Government; Chair of NIST's Information Security and Privacy Advisory Board
Larry Clinton, President and CEO, Internet Security Alliance
Tom Gann, Vice President of Government Relations, McAfee

Seymour E. Goodman, Professor of International Affairs and Computing, Sam Nunn School of International Affairs, College of Computing at Georgia Institute of Technology

Susan Landau, Independent Scholar

James Lewis, Director and Senior Fellow of Technology and Public Policy, Center for Strategic and International Studies

Herbert Lin, Chief Scientist, Computer Science and Telecommunications Board, National Research Council of the National Academies

Randy V. Sabett, Counsel, ZwillGen LLP

Peter Weinberger, Senior Software Engineer, Google

CIO Survey Participants

Darren B. Ash, U.S. Nuclear Regulatory Commission

Frank Baitman, Department of Health and Human Services

Roger W. Baker, Department of Veterans Affairs

Danny A. Harris, Department of Education

Bernard J. Mazer, Department of the Interior

Matthew E. Perry, Office of Personnel Management

Tim Schmidt, Department of Transportation

Richard Spires, Department of Homeland Security

Simon Szykman, Department of Commerce

Steven C. Taylor, Department of State

Eric Won, Small Business Administration

RELATED GAO PRODUCTS

Information Security: Better Implementation of Controls for Mobile Devices Should Be Encouraged. GAO-12-757. Washington, D.C.: September 18, 2012.

Medical Devices: FDA Should Expand Its Consideration of Information Security for Certain Types of Devices. GAO-12-816. Washington, D.C.: August 31, 2012.

Bureau of the Public Debt: Areas for Improvement in Information Systems Controls. GAO-12-616. Washington, D.C.: May 24, 2012.

Cybersecurity: Challenges in Securing the Electricity Grid. GAO-12-926T. Washington, D.C.: July 17, 2012.

Electronic Warfare: DOD Actions Needed to Strengthen Management and Oversight. GAO-12-479. Washington, D.C.: July 9, 2012.

Information Security: Cyber Threats Facilitate Ability to Commit Economic Espionage. GAO-12-876T. Washington, D.C.: June 28, 2012

Cybersecurity: Threats Impacting the Nation. GAO-12-666T. Washington, D.C.: April 24, 2012.

IT Supply Chain: National Security-Related Agencies Need to Better Address Risks. GAO-12-361. Washington, D.C.: March 23, 2012.

Information Security: IRS Needs to Further Enhance Internal Control over Financial Reporting and Taxpayer Data. GAO-12-393. Washington, D.C.: March 16, 2012.

Cybersecurity: Challenges in Securing the Modernized Electricity Grid. GAO-12-507T. Washington, D.C.: February 28, 2012.

Critical Infrastructure Protection: Cybersecurity Guidance Is Available, but More Can Be Done to Promote Its Use. GAO-12-92. Washington, D.C.: December 9, 2011.

Cybersecurity Human Capital: Initiatives Need Better Planning and Coordination. GAO-12-8. Washington, D.C.: November 29, 2011.

Information Security: Additional Guidance Needed to Address Cloud Computing Concerns. GAO-12-130T. Washington, D.C.: October 6, 2011.

Information Security: Weaknesses Continue Amid New Federal Efforts to Implement Requirements. GAO-12-137. Washington, D.C.: October 3, 2011.

Personal ID Verification: Agencies Should Set a Higher Priority on Using the Capabilities of Standardized Identification Cards. GAO-11-751. Washington, D.C.: September 20, 2011.

Information Security: FDIC Has Made Progress, but Further Actions Are Needed to Protect Financial Data. GAO-11-708. Washington, D.C.: August 12, 2011.

Cybersecurity: Continued Attention Needed to Protect Our Nation's Critical Infrastructure. GAO-11-865T. Washington, D.C.: July 26, 2011.

Defense Department Cyber Efforts: DOD Faces Challenges in Its Cyber Activities. GAO-11-75. Washington, D.C.: July 25, 2011.

Information Security: State Has Taken Steps to Implement a Continuous Monitoring Application, but Key Challenges Remain. GAO-11-149. Washington, D.C.: July 8, 2011.

Social Media: Federal Agencies Need Policies and Procedures for Managing and Protecting Information They Access and Disseminate. GAO-11-605. Washington, D.C.: June 28, 2011.

Cybersecurity: Continued Attention Needed to Protect Our Nation's Critical

Infrastructure and Federal Information Systems. GAO-11-463T. Washington, D.C.: March 16, 2011.

Information Security: IRS Needs to Enhance Internal Control Over Financial Reporting and Taxpayer Data. GAO-11-308. Washington, D.C.: March 15, 2011.

High-Risk Series: An Update. GAO-11-278. Washington, D.C.: February 16, 2011.

Electricity Grid Modernization: Progress Being Made on Cybersecurity Guidelines, but Key Challenges Remain to Be Addressed. GAO-11-117. Washington, D.C.: January 12, 2011.

Information Security: National Nuclear Security Administration Needs to Improve Contingency Planning for Its Classified Supercomputing Operations. GAO-11-67. Washington, D.C.: December 9, 2010.

Information Security: Federal Agencies Have Taken Steps to Secure Wireless Networks, but Further Actions Can Mitigate Risk. GAO-11-43. Washington, D.C.: November 30, 2010.

Information Security: Federal Deposit Insurance Corporation Needs to Mitigate Control Weaknesses. GAO-11-29. Washington, D.C.: November 30, 2010.

Information Security: National Archives and Records Administration Needs to Implement Key Program Elements and Controls. GAO-11-20. Washington, D.C.: October 21, 2010.

Cyberspace Policy: Executive Branch Is Making Progress Implementing 2009 Policy Review Recommendations, but Sustained Leadership Is Needed. GAO-11-24. Washington, D.C.: October 6, 2010.

Information Security: Progress Made on Harmonizing Policies and Guidance for National Security and Non-National Security Systems. GAO-10-916. Washington, D.C.: September 15, 2010.

Information Management: Challenges in Federal Agencies' Use of Web 2.0 Technologies. GAO-10-872T. Washington, D.C.: July 22, 2010.

Critical Infrastructure Protection: Key Private and Public Cyber Expectations Need to Be Consistently Addressed. GAO-10-628. Washington, D.C.: July 15, 2010.

Cyberspace: United States Faces Challenges in Addressing Global Cybersecurity and Governance. GAO-10-606. Washington, D.C.: July 2, 2010.

Information Security: Governmentwide Guidance Needed to Assist Agencies in Implementing Cloud Computing. GAO-10-855T. Washington, D.C.: July 1, 2010.

Cybersecurity: Continued Attention Is Needed to Protect Federal Information Systems from Evolving Threats. GAO-10-834T. Washington, D.C.: June 16, 2010.

Cybersecurity: Key Challenges Need to Be Addressed to Improve Research and Development. GAO-10-466. Washington, D.C.: June 3, 2010.

Information Security: Federal Guidance Needed to Address Control Issues with Implementing Cloud Computing. GAO-10-513. Washington, D.C.: May 27, 2010.

Information Security: Opportunities Exist for the Federal Housing Finance Agency to Improve Control. GAO-10-528. Washington, D.C.: April 30, 2010.

Information Security: Concerted Response Needed to Resolve Persistent Weaknesses. GAO-10-536T. Washington, D.C.: March 24, 2010.

Information Security: IRS Needs to Continue to Address Significant Weaknesses. GAO-10-355. Washington, D.C.: March 19, 2010.

Information Security: Concerted Effort Needed to Consolidate and Secure Internet Connections at Federal Agencies. GAO-10-237. Washington, D.C.: March 12, 2010.

Information Security: Agencies Need to Implement Federal Desktop Core Configuration Requirements. GAO-10-202. Washington, D.C.: March 12, 2010.

Cybersecurity: Progress Made but Challenges Remain in Defining and Coordinating the Comprehensive National Initiative. GAO-10-338. Washington, D.C.: March 5, 2010.

Critical Infrastructure Protection: Update to National Infrastructure Protection Plan Includes Increased Emphasis on Risk Management and Resilience. GAO-10-296. Washington, D.C.: March 5, 2010.

Department of Veterans Affairs' Implementation of Information Security Education Assistance Program. GAO-10-170R. Washington, D.C.: December 18, 2009.

Cybersecurity: Continued Efforts Are Needed to Protect Information Systems from Evolving Threats. GAO-10-230T. Washington, D.C.: November 17, 2009.

Information Security: Concerted Effort Needed to Improve Federal Performance Measures. GAO-10-159T. Washington, D.C.: October 29, 2009.

Critical Infrastructure Protection: OMB Leadership Needed to Strengthen Agency Planning Efforts to Protect Federal Cyber Assets. GAO-10-148. Washington, D.C.: October 15, 2009.

Information Security: NASA Needs to Remedy Vulnerabilities in Key Networks. GAO-10-4. Washington, D.C.: October 15, 2009.

Information Security: Actions Needed to Better Manage, Protect, and Sustain Improvements to Los Alamos National Laboratory's Classified Computer Network. GAO-10-28. Washington, D.C.: October 14, 2009.

Critical Infrastructure Protection: Current Cyber Sector-Specific Planning Approach Needs Reassessment. GAO-09-969. Washington, D.C.: September 24, 2009.

Information Security: Federal Information Security Issues. GAO-09-817R. Washington, D.C.: June 30, 2009.

Information Security: Concerted Effort Needed to Improve Federal Performance Measures. GAO-09-617. Washington, D.C.: September 14, 2009.

Information Security: Agencies Continue to Report Progress, but Need to Mitigate Persistent Weaknesses. GAO-09-546. Washington, D.C.: July 17, 2009.

National Cybersecurity Strategy: Key Improvements Are Needed to Strengthen the Nation's Posture. GAO-09-432T. Washington, D.C.: March 10, 2009.

I*nformation Technology: Federal Laws, Regulations, and Mandatory Standards to Securing Private Sector Information Technology Systems and Data in Critical Infrastructure Sectors*. GAO-08-1075R. Washington, D.C.: September 16, 2008.

Cyber Analysis and Warning: DHS Faces Challenges in Establishing a Comprehensive National Capability. GAO-08-588. Washington, D.C.: July 31, 2008.

Information Security: Federal Agency Efforts to Encrypt Sensitive Information Are Under Way, but Work Remains. GAO-08-525. Washington, D.C.: June 27, 2008.

Privacy: Lessons Learned about Data Breach Notification. GAO-07-657. Washington, D.C.: April 30, 2007.

End Notes

[1] Critical infrastructure includes systems and assets so vital to the United States that their incapacity or destruction would have a debilitating impact on national security.

[2] This includes the Federal Information Security Management Act of 2002 (FISMA), the Homeland Security Act of 2002, and the Homeland Security Presidential Directive 7, among other laws and directives.

[3] The 24 major departments and agencies are the Departments of Agriculture, Commerce, Defense, Education, Energy, Health and Human Services, Homeland Security, Housing and Urban Development, the Interior, Justice, Labor, State, Transportation, the Treasury, and Veterans Affairs; the Environmental Protection Agency, General Services Administration, National Aeronautics and Space Administration, National Science Foundation, Nuclear Regulatory Commission, Office of Personnel Management, Small Business Administration, Social Security Administration, and U.S. Agency for International Development.

[4] President Barack Obama, "Remarks by the President on Securing Our Nation's Cyber Infrastructure" (Washington, D.C.: May 29, 2009).

[5] James R. Clapper, Director of National Intelligence, "Unclassified Statement for the Record on the Worldwide Threat Assessment of the US Intelligence Community for the Senate Select Committee on Intelligence" (January 31, 2012).

[6] Secretary of Defense Leon E. Panetta, "Remarks by Secretary Panetta on Cybersecurity to the Business Executives for National Security, New York City" (New York, NY: Oct. 11, 2012).

[7] See GAO, *High Risk Series: An Update*, GAO-11-278 (Washington, D.C.: February 2011).

[8] Malware is malicious software and is defined as programs that are designed to carry out annoying or harmful actions. Once installed, malware can often masquerade as useful programs or be embedded into useful programs so that users are induced into activating the program, spreading itself onto other devices.

[9] An incident is categorized as "improper usage" if a person violates acceptable computing use policies.

[10] Paul K. Martin, Inspector General, National Aeronautics and Space Administration, "NASA Cybersecurity: An Examination of the Agency's Information Security," testimony before the Subcommittee on Investigations and Oversight, Committee on Science, Space, and Technology, House of Representatives (Washington, D.C.: Feb. 29, 2012).

[11] The RSA SecureID system is the most widely used two-factor authentication solution providing secure access to remote and mobile users.

[12] The Federal Retirement Thrift Investment Board is an independent agency in the executive branch governed by five presidentially appointed board members and is responsible for administering the Thrift Savings Plan (TSP) and managing the investments of the Thrift Savings Fund.

[13] TSP is a tax-deferred defined contribution savings plan for federal employees similar to the 401(k) plans offered by private employers.

[14] Title III of the E-Government Act of 2002, Pub. L. No. 107-347, Dec. 17, 2002; 44 U.S.C 3541, et seq. This report discusses FISMA because it is the primary law specifying federal agencies' cybersecurity responsibilities. Other laws give federal agencies general responsibilities that can include cybersecurity-related duties. For example, the Federal Bureau of Investigation is responsible for detecting and prosecuting crimes under 28 U.S.C. § 533, which can include cybercrimes, and 50 U.S.C. ch. 15 addresses national security responsibilities of national defense and intelligence agencies, which can also include cyber-related threats to national security.

[15] As defined in FISMA, the term "national security system" means any information system used by or on behalf of a federal agency that (1) involves intelligence activities, national security-related cryptologic activities, command and control of military forces, or equipment that is an integral part of a weapon or weapons system, or is critical to the direct fulfillment of military or intelligence missions (excluding systems used for routine administrative and business applications); or (2) is protected at all times by procedures established for handling classified national security information. See 44 U.S.C. § 3542(b)(2).

[16] FISMA limits NIST to developing, in conjunction with DOD and the National Security Agency, guidelines for agencies on identifying an information system as a national security system, and for ensuring that NIST standards and guidelines are complementary with standards and guidelines developed for national security systems.

[17] Pub. L. No. 107-305 (Nov. 27, 2002); 15 U.S.C.§ 7406(c).

[18] In December 2009, a Special Assistant to the President was appointed as Cybersecurity Coordinator to address the recommendations made in the Cyberspace Policy Review, including coordinating interagency cybersecurity policies and strategies and developing a comprehensive national strategy to secure the nation's digital infrastructure.

[19] OMB, Memorandum M-10-28, *Clarifying Cybersecurity Responsibilities and Activities of the Executive Office of the President and the Department of Homeland Security* (Washington, D.C.: July 6, 2010).

[20] As used in OMB M-10-28, the term cybersecurity applies to activities undertaken to provide information security as defined by FISMA.

[21] Fiscal year 2011 reporting instructions for the Federal Information Security Management Act and agency privacy management were issued by DHS, as Federal Information Security Memorandum (FISM) 11-02 (Aug. 24, 2011), and by OMB, as M-11-33 (Sept. 14, 2011). Fiscal year 2012 reporting instructions were issued by DHS, as FISM 12-02 (Feb. 15, 2012), and by OMB, as M-12-20 (Sept. 27, 2012). While identically titled, these memos varied in content.

[22] National Security Directive 42, *National Policy for the Security of National Security Telecommunications and Information Systems* (July 5, 1990).

[23] See GAO, *Defense Department Cyber Efforts: DOD Faces Challenges in its Cyber Activities,* GAO-11-75 (Washington, D.C.: July 25, 2011).

[24] See GAO, *Information Security: Progress Made in Harmonizing Policies and Guidance for National Security and Non-National Security Systems*, GAO-10-916 (Washington, D.C.: Sept. 15, 2010).

[25] See GAO, *Critical Infrastructure Protection: Cybersecurity Guidance Is Available, but More Can Be Done to Promote Its Use* (Washington, D.C.: Dec. 9, 2011) for a more in- depth discussion on the responsibilities of the federal government as they relate to critical infrastructure protection.

[26] Sector-specific agencies are federal agencies designated to be focal points for specific critical infrastructure sectors.

[27] S.3414, among other things, also addressed cybersecurity workforce issues, cybersecurity research and development, and critical infrastructure protection.

[28] S.3342, among other things, also addressed cybersecurity workforce issues, cybersecurity research and development, and cybercrime.

[29] H.R.1136, among other things, also addressed supply chain security and critical infrastructure protection.

[30] GPRA, Pub. L. No. 103-62, 107 Stat. 285 (1993).

[31] The White House, *National Strategy for Trusted Identities in Cyberspace: Enhancing Online Choice, Efficiency, Security, and Privacy* (Washington, D.C.: April 2011).

[32] The strategy defines an "Identity Ecosystem" as an online environment where individuals and organizations will be able to trust each other because they follow agreed upon standards to obtain and authenticate their digital identities—and the digital identities of devices.

[33] OSTP, an office within the Executive Office of the President, advises the President on science and technology issues. It also coordinates related polices and R&D strategies across federal agencies, including through the National Science and Technology Council.

[34] National Science and Technology Council, *Trustworthy Cyberspace: Strategic Plan for the Federal Cybersecurity Research and Development Program* (Washington, D.C.: Dec. 6, 2011).

[35] The White House, *International Strategy for Cyberspace: Prosperity, Security, and Openness in a Networked World* (Washington, D.C.: May 2011).

[36] Pub. L. No. 111-352, 124 Stat. 3866, 3873 (2011).

[37] DHS, *National Infrastructure Protection Plan, Partnering to Enhance Protection and Resiliency* (Washington, D.C.: January 2009).

[38] GAO, *Cyberspace Policy: Executive Branch is Making Progress Implementing 2009 Policy Review Recommendations, but Sustained Leadership Is Needed*, GAO-11-24 (Washington, D.C.: Oct. 6, 2010).

[39] The White House, "Fact Sheet: The Administration's Cybersecurity Accomplishments" (May 12, 2011), accessed on July 26, 2012, http://www.whitehouse.gov/the-press-office/2011/05/12/fact-sheet-administrations-cybersecurity-accomplishments.

[40] GAO, *Combating Terrorism: Evaluation of Selected Characteristics in National Strategies Related to Terrorism*, GAO-04-408T (Washington, D.C.: Feb. 3, 2004).

[41] The *National Strategy for Trusted Identities in Cyberspace* includes interim benchmarks (3-5 years) and longer-term benchmarks (10 years) for determining whether the strategy was successful.

[42] DHS Office of Inspector General, *Planning, Management, and Systems Issues Hinder DHS' Efforts to Protect Cyberspace and the Nation's Cyber Infrastructure*, OIG-11-89 (Washington, D.C.: June 2011).

[43] GAO, *Homeland Defense: DOD Needs to Address Gaps in Homeland Defense and Civil Support Guidance,* GAO-13-128 (Washington, D.C.: Oct. 24, 2012).

[44] Department of Defense Directive 5111.18, *Assistant Secretary of Defense for Global Strategic Affairs* (June 13, 2011); and Department of Defense Directive 5111.13, *Assistant Secretary of Defense for Homeland Defense and Americas' Security Affairs* (Jan. 16, 2009).

[45] GAO, *Cybersecurity: Progress Made but Challenges Remain in Defining and Coordinating the Comprehensive National Initiative*, GAO-10-338 (Washington, D.C.: Mar. 5, 2010).

[46] DHS issued the *Blueprint for a Secure Cyber Future* to establish a plan of action for the department to implement the National Security Strategy and to achieve other DHS cybersecurity goals.

[47] NIST, *Managing Information Security Risk: Organization, Mission, and InformationSystem View,* NIST Special Publication 800-39 (Gaithersburg, Md.: March 2011); *Guide for Applying the Risk Management Framework to Federal Information Systems: A Security Life Cycle Approach*, NIST Special Publication 800-37 Revision 1 (Gaithersburg, Md.: February 2010); and *Guide for Conducting Risk Assessments*, NIST Special Publication 800-30 Revision 1 (Gaithersburg, Md.: September 2012).

[48] GAO, *Information Security: Weaknesses Continue Amid New Federal Efforts to Implement Requirements*, GAO-12-137 (Washington, D.C.: Oct. 3, 2011).

[49] NIST released an update of this publication in May 2010. An initial public draft for comment of the fourth revision of this publication was released in February 2012.

[50] Each inspector general is asked to assess his or her agency's information security programs in 11 areas: risk management, configuration management, incident response and reporting, security training, plans of actions and milestones, remote access management, identity and access management, continuous monitoring management, contingency planning, contractor systems, and security capital planning.

[51] GAO-12-137.

[52] GAO, *Information Security: State Has Taken Steps to Implement a Continuous Monitoring Application, but Key Challenges Remain*, GAO-11-149 (Washington, D.C.: July 8, 2011).

[53] GAO, *Critical Infrastructure Protection: Cybersecurity Guidance Is Available, but More Can Be Done to Promote Its Use*, GAO-12-92 (Washington, D.C.: Dec. 9, 2011). In commenting on a draft of the report, an Oil and Natural Gas Subsector Coordinating Council representative familiar with cybersecurity-related regulation stated that entities in the oil and natural gas subsector that have high-risk chemical facilities are subject to Chemical Facility Anti-Terrorism Standards. Facilities covered by this standard are required to implement measures to deter cyber sabotage, and prevent unauthorized onsite or remote access to critical process controls systems, critical business systems, and sensitive computerized systems.

[54] An electronic security perimeter is the logical border surrounding a network to which critical cyber assets are connected and for which access is controlled.

[55] DHS, National Cyber Security Division, Control Systems Security Program, *Catalog of Control Systems Security: Recommendations for Standards Developers* (April 2011).

[56] ISACs by definition are critical infrastructure sector-specific, trusted communities of security specialists that identify, analyze, and share information; collaborate on threats, incidents, vulnerabilities, and best practices; and work to protect their respective industries from cyber and physical threats.

[57] The DHS National Exercise Program provides a framework for prioritizing and coordinating federal, regional, and state exercise activities, without replacing any individual department or agency exercises. The program enables federal, state, and local departments and agencies to align their exercise programs.

[58] Cyber Storm is DHS's biennial exercise series that provides the framework to strengthen cyber preparedness in the public and private sectors.

[59] "EINSTEIN" is a suite of capabilities that monitor and analyze cyber threat data transiting to and from federal civilian government networks.

[60] State and major urban area fusion centers serve as focal points within the state and local environment for the receipt, analysis, gathering, and sharing of threat-related information between the federal government and state, local, tribal, territorial, and private sector partners.

[61] JACKE is a classified forum for federal departments and agencies to exchange cyber threat and defense information.

[62] The Government Forum of Incident Response and Security Teams is a group of technical and tactical practitioners from incident response and security response teams from federal, state, and local agencies responsible for securing government information technology systems and providing private sector support.

[63] DHS Office of Inspector General, *U.S. Computer Emergency Readiness Team Makes Progress in Security Cyberspace, but Challenges Remain,* OIG-10-94 (Washington, D.C.: June 2010).

[64] Products US-CERT disseminates include: Situational Awareness Reports, Critical Infrastructure Information Notices, Federal Information Notices, Early Warning Indicator Notices, and Malware Initial Findings Reports.

[65] GAO, *Cyber Analysis and Warning: DHS Faces Challenges in Establishing a Comprehensive National Capability*, GAO-08-588 (Washington D.C.: July 31, 2008), and *Critical Infrastructure Protection: Key Private and Public Cyber Expectations Need to Be Consistently Addressed*, GAO-10-628 (Washington, D.C.: July 15, 2010).

[66] DHS Office of Inspector General, *Relationships between Fusion Centers and Emergency Operations Centers*, OIG-12-15 (Washington, D.C.: December 2011).

[67] A tear-line report contains a physical line on an intelligence message or document which separates categories of information that have been approved for disclosure and release. Normally, the information below the tear line has been cleared for disclosure or release.

[68] DHS Office of Inspector General, *Review of the Department of Homeland Security's Capability to Share Cyber Threat Information* (Redacted), OIG-11-117 (Washington, D.C.: September 2011).

[69] DHS Office of Inspector General, *Relationships Between Fusion Centers and Emergency Operations Centers*, OIG-12-15 (Washington, D.C.: December 2011).

[70] Statement of Richard L. Skinner Former Inspector General U.S. Department of Homeland Security before the Senate Committee on Homeland Security and Governmental Affairs, "The Future of Homeland Security: The Evolution of the Homeland Security Department's Roles and Missions" (Washington, D.C.: July 12, 2012).

[71] DHS Office of Inspector General, *U.S. Computer Emergency Readiness Team Makes Progress in Security Cyberspace, but Challenges Remain,* OIG-10-94 (Washington, D.C.: June 2010).

[72] DHS Office of Inspector General, *DHS Can Strengthen Its International Cybersecurity Programs* (Redacted), OIG-12-112 (Washington, D.C.: August 2012).

[73] GAO-08-588.

[74] Statement for the Record of DHS representatives Roberta Stempfley and Sean P. McGurk before the United States House of Representatives Committee on Energy and Commerce Subcommittee on Oversight and Investigations (Washington D.C.: July 26, 2011).

[75] GAO-08-588.

[76] DHS Office of Inspector General, OIG-10-94.

[77] GAO, *Human Capital: Key Principles for Effective Strategic Workforce Planning,* GAO-04-39 (Washington, D.C.: Dec. 11, 2003); *A Model of Strategic Human Capital Management,* GAO-02-373SP (Washington, D.C.: March 2002); and *Human Capital: A Self-Assessment Checklist for Agency Leaders,* GAO/OCG-00-14G (Washington, D.C.: September 2000).

[78] OPM, *Human Capital Assessment and Accountability Framework—Systems, Standards, and Metrics* (http://www.opm.gov/hcaaf_resource_center/2-2.asp).

[79] Centers for Information Technology Excellence were meant to train and certify current federal IT personnel and help maintain their skill levels throughout their careers.

[80] GAO-10-338.

[81] GAO, *Cybersecurity Human Capital: Initiatives Need Better Planning and Coordination*, GAO-12-8 (Washington, D.C.: Nov. 29, 2011).

[82] GAO-12-8.

[83] The interagency working group coordinates R&D activities.

[84] National Science and Technology Council, *Trustworthy Cyberspace: Strategic Plan for the Federal Cybersecurity Research and Development Program* (Washington, D.C.: Dec. 6, 2011).

[85] OSTP's Subcommittee on Networking and Information Technology Research and Development is a multiagency body that coordinates cybersecurity R&D.

[86] GAO, *Cybersecurity: Key Challenges Need to Be Addressed to Improve Research and Development,* GAO-10-466 (Washington, D.C.: June 3, 2010).

[87] GAO, *Electronic Government Act: Agencies Have Implemented Most Provisions, but Key Areas of Attention Remain*, GAO-12-782 (Washington, D.C.: Sept. 12, 2012).

[88] Science.gov was intended to be the R&D repository and provide the public and agencies with information about federally funded R&D activities through links to science websites and scientific databases.

[89] The R&D dashboard currently provides information on federal investments in research and development from the National Institutes of Health and the National Science Foundation from 2000 to 2009.

[90] GAO-10-338.

[91] GAO, *Cyberspace: United States Faces Challenges in Addressing Global Cybersecurity and Governance*, GAO-10-606 (Washington, D.C.: July 2, 2010).

[92] These strategies include the *National Plan for Information Systems Protection, National Strategy to Secure Cyberspace, Comprehensive National Cybersecurity Initiative, White House Cyberspace Policy Review, National Strategy for Trusted Identities in Cyberspace,* and *International Strategy for Cyberspace.*

[93] GAO, *Combating Terrorism: Evaluation of Selected Characteristics in National Strategies Related to Terrorism*, GAO-04-408T (Washington, D.C.: Feb. 3, 2004).

[94] Anyone employed by the federal government at the time of selection was excluded.

[95] We invited the lead individual for organizations that may have had multiple individuals listed (e.g., Carnegie Mellon and the Center for Internet Security).

[96] Being listed as a member of the Computer Science and Telecommunications Board and one or more of its committees was counted as a single source. Similarly, testifying at multiple congressional hearings also counted as a single source.

In: U.S. National Cybersecurity
Editor: Grace Powers
ISBN: 978-1-63321-831-4

Chapter 2

IMMEDIATE OPPORTUNITIES FOR STRENGTHENING THE NATION'S CYBERSECURITY*

President's Council of Advisors on Science and Technology

I. SUMMARY OF FINDINGS AND RECOMMENDATIONS

PCAST's report can be summarized by one overarching finding and six additional numbered findings. Recommendations follow from each of those six. The main report text gives background and further elaboration.

Overarching Finding: Cybersecurity will not be achieved by a collection of static precautions that, if taken by Government and industry organizations, will make them secure. Rather, it requires a set of processes that continuously couple information about an evolving threat to defensive reactions and responses.

The additional findings and associated recommendations are as follows.

* This is an edited, reformatted and augmented version --------------, dated November 2013.

Finding 1: The Federal Government rarely follows accepted best practices. It needs to lead by example and accelerate its efforts to make routine cyberattacks more difficult by implementing best practices for its own systems.

Recommendations

- Phase out within two years the use of unsupported and insecure operating systems, such as Windows XP, in favor of modern systems, such as current versions of Windows, Linux, and Mac OS.
- Encourage the universal adoption of the Trusted Platform Module (TPM; an industry-standard microchip designed to provide basic security-related functions, primarily involving encryption keys), including for phones and tablets.
- Encourage the universal adoption of the latest, most secure browsers to facilitate prevention of identity theft.
- Move toward nationwide availability of proofed identities for people, roles, devices, and soft ware. While voluntary in the private sector, these should be mandatory for transactions and data exchanges among Federal users.
- Encourage effective Federal use of automatically updating software, including cloud-hosted software, both for COTS and GOTS[1] products.

Finding 2: Many private-sector entities come under some form of Federal regulation for reasons not directly related to national security. In many such cases there is opportunity, fully consistent with the intent of the existing enabling legislation, for promoting and achieving best practices in cybersecurity.

Recommendations

- Within already regulated industries, the regulator should require not a specific list of cyber security measures but rather an auditable process by which cybersecurity best practices are adopted and continually improved.
- The President should strongly encourage independent regulatory agencies to adopt regulations that require self-reporting of continuous-

improvement practices along these same lines. In particular, the Securities and Exchange Commission (SEC) should mandate, for publicly held companies, the disclosure, as investment risks, of cybersecurity risk factors that go beyond current materiality tests.

Finding 3: Industry-driven, but third-party-audited, continuous-improvement processes are more likely to create an effective cybersecurity culture than are Government-mandated, static lists of security measures.

Recommendation

- For the private sector, Government's role should be to encourage continuously improving, consensus-based standards and transparent reporting of whether those standards are being met by individual private-sector entities.

Finding 4: To improve the capacity to respond in real time, cyberthreat data need to be shared more extensively among private-sector entities and—in appropriate circumstances and with publicly understood interfaces—between private-sector entities and Government.

Recommendation

- The Federal Government should act to facilitate the establishment of private-sector partner ships for the real-time exchange of threat data among potentially vulnerable private-sector entities. Data flows among these private-sector entities should not and would not be accessible by the Government. The Government might participate in establishing protocols, or providing technology, for how the data are utilized by the private sector for cyberdefense. The protocols or technology utilized should have sufficient transparency to mitigate legitimate concerns about inappropriate Government access to private data.

Finding 5: Internet Service Providers are well-positioned to contribute to rapid improvements in cybersecurity through real-time action.

Recommendations

- The Federal Government should establish policies that describe the desired behavior by ISPs as best (or minimum-acceptable) practices.
- The National Institute of Standards and Technology (NIST) should work with ISPs towards establishing standards for voluntary measures by which ISPs can alert users and direct them to appropriate resources when their machines or devices are known to be compromised.

Finding 6: Future architectures will need to start with the premise that each part of a system must be designed to operate in a hostile environment. Research is needed to foster systems with dynamic, real-time defenses to complement hardening approaches.

Recommendations

- The Nation's research universities and industry laboratories should be more directly partnered in the creation of high-assurance computing systems, including hardware, firmware, and the complete software stack.
- An independent organization should be tasked with the development of certifiable maturity levels with respect to threat-aware design processes for companies that design hardware and software.
- The Nation should invest in high-risk, high-return basic research with a 10to20year time horizon that, if successful, could fundamentally transform the future cybersecurity landscape.

II. INTRODUCTION

Cyberthreats span the range from cybercrime (with global economic damage estimated at $100 billion to $1 trillion annually[2]) to potentially devastating cyberattacks against U.S. critical infrastructure, both civilian and military. In peacetime, cyberspace without adequate cybersecurity is a sanctuary from which criminal hackers, spammers, viruses, botnets,[3] and other cyberthreats prey daily and openly on U.S. individuals and organizations. The Nation's capacity for innovation and commerce, including time-to-market advantages for commercial products and unique U.S. technologies for national defense, is drained by cyber industrial espionage and theft. In wartime, cyberspace can become another platform from which strategic attacks can be launched against the U.S. homeland and U.S. allies and interests abroad; cyber operations against U.S. forces can severely degrade military capabilities. Over the long term, national security depends on sustained economic security. If the Nation does not move aggressively to defend against these cybersecurity-induced disruptions and losses, that economic security will be susceptible to disruption on a timescale and breadth previously not imagined, due to the pervasive dependencies our society now has on information technologies of large scale.

The Internet provides unprecedented scalability of actions by a single individual,[4] non-state group, or hostile nation. A single computer on the Internet can easily attack millions of other computers. The Internet protocol is designed to be globally interoperable with a range of devices—one of the key reasons for its explosive growth, adoption, and pace of innovation—but as a result it allows promiscuous connections to be made without authentication. Indeed, the Internet protocol was designed virtually assuming that all users were trustworthy. And, far beyond the scale of a single machine, botnets enable hostile actions by millions of machines simultaneously.

Steady progress has been made in the domains of discovery, remediation, and hardening in the traditional computing environment, but a tidal wave of new devices, from smartphones and computerized in-car systems to a wide range of smart sensors and other objects, is coming online. Few of these are being introduced with acceptable levels of cybersecurity. In a globally connected society, users of compromised machines and devices put not only their own systems and information at risk but also those of other Internet users. Compromised devices are vectors for the additional spread of malware, and they can be recruited into botnets and other systematic mechanisms for immediate or eventual (weeks, months, or years later) massive cyberattacks on U.S. companies or U.S. critical infrastructure.

The heterogeneous ownership and control of devices connected to the Internet makes it difficult-to impossible to implement security fixes rapidly and uniformly. The highly cross-connected (and to some extent dynamic) nature of the Internet's interior dictates that most security measures need to be applied at or near the endpoints. The challenge is that they must be adopted by literally billions of users and devices. There are few, if any, interior chokepoints at which it is possible to apply security measures with high effectiveness. For example, not all packets pass through Tier 1 (top-level

Internet network) backbone interconnects; those that do are frequently encrypted, defeating most forms of security that depend on deep-packet inspection; not all Tier 1 providers are U.S. corporations; and, in any case, the U.S. Government largely lacks authorities to compel actions within the private sector.

These Realities Imply an Overarching Finding

Cybersecurity will not be achieved by a collection of static precautions that, if taken by Government and industry organizations, will make them secure. Rather, it requires a set of processes that must continuously couple information about an evolving threat to defensive reactions and responses.

When this feedback loop has a timescale of weeks or years, it may be called "hardening," which is the essence of currently accepted "best practices." When it has a timescale of sub-second to minutes, it may be called "dynamic, real-time response," or "fast reactive response," or "network-based defense." But both need to be pieces of a single, unified, national cyberdefense architecture whose top-level paradigm is that flows of information about threats are able to trigger appropriate responsive actions. A national cybersecurity policy needs to be comprehensive in addressing all of the relevant timescales. The emphasis of this report, however, is largely—though not exclusively—on measures such as hardening and other best practices that unfold on the longer timescales.

III. Hardening Efforts Need Attention

Much can be done to make attacks against the U.S. Government, industry, and individuals more difficult and to decrease both the actual and perceived lawlessness of the Internet.

In this activity, Government's role is to encourage and facilitate the broad adoption of known best practices for information technology (IT) management. Several initiatives in President Obama's first term were of this character: the trusted identities initiative,[5] the three identified priorities for Federal cybersecurity,[6] the consolidation of Federal access points, the electricity-sector maturity model,[7] and voluntary steps taken to counter botnets.[8] In the second term, the President also signed Executive Order 13636[9] and Presidential Policy Directive 21,[10] which together supported a number of Executive actions focused on enhancing critical infrastructure cybersecurity, partnership, and standards development.

These are individually useful actions, but there is both need and opportunity for more assertive White House actions that accelerate progress.

Finding: The Federal Government rarely follows accepted best practices. It needs to lead by example and accelerate its efforts to make cyberattacks more difficult by implementing harden- ing practices for its own systems.

PCAST's Recommendations in this Area Are

- Announce a firm commitment to phase out within two years use by the Federal Government of insecure and potentially unsupported operating systems, such as Windows XP, in favor of modern systems, such as current versions of Windows, Linux, and Mac OS. These are vastly more secure, and they are likely to be more effectively patched in response to new threats. There is simply no excuse for the Federal Government to be such a poor leader by example. This action was also recommended by the Internet Security and Privacy Advisory Board (established by the Computer Security Act of 1987) by letter to the Office of Management and Budget (OMB) dated March 30, 2012.
- Take steps, for example by Federal procurement preference, that encourage the universal adoption of the Trusted Platform Module (TPM), an industry-standard microchip designed to provide basic security-related functions, primarily involving encryption keys, including for phones and tablets. Computers and devices that incorporate a TPM are able to create cryptographic keys and encrypt them so they can be decrypted only by the TPM. A TPM provides this limited but fundamental set of capabilities that higher layers of cybersecurity can then leverage. Today, TPMs are present in many laptop and desktop personal computers. They are leveraged by enterprises for tasks like secure disk encryption, but they have yet to be incorporated to any significant extent in smartphones, game consoles, televisions, in-car computer systems, and other computerized devices and industrial control systems. This needs to

happen for such devices to be "trustworthy" constituents of what is an increasingly interconnected device ecosystem.

- Similarly, encourage the universal adoption of the latest, most secure browsers to facilitate prevention of identity theft. The majority of attacks on computers involve password guessing and "phishing" (in which false information is placed in front of the user to motivate unintended disclosure of sensitive information). Behind the scenes, modern browsers such as Chrome, Safari, and Internet Explorer check for the most common ways of stealing information, and they also help verify that software being downloaded is from a secure site.
- Move toward nationwide availability of proofed identities for people, roles, devices, and soft ware. The April 2011 White House paper, "National Strategy for Trusted Identities in Cyberspace," offers an overview of identity issues, although its proposed "identity ecosystem" is dauntingly complex and has not yet seen significant adoption. For immediate impact, we recommend instead focusing on readily implementable approaches to creating trusted identities. One such approach is claims-based identity, which grants individuals multiple identities they can use in specific circumstances and is one way to avoid the privacy and civil-liberty issues inherent in schemes such as national identity cards. A claims-based model passes specific "claims" about an individual (e.g., date of birth, age) instead of that individual's "whole" identity (e.g., all the data on a driver's license). While voluntary in the private sector, use of proofed identities should be mandatory for transactions and data exchanges within the Federal Government.
- Encourage Federal use of automatically-updating software both for commercial and government off-the-shelf software (COTS and GOTS), and provide or endorse standards (e.g., created by the National Institute of Standards and Technology (NIST) or via the private-sector standards setting process) for ensuring the transactional security of such updates. Cloud-hosted software, because it is updated uniformly for all users, is desirable in this regard. While some new attacks against software will succeed ("fool me once, shame on you"), old attacks should never succeed ("fool me twice, shame on me"). Leading by example, the Federal Government should embrace this principle.

IV. A National Strategy Can Accelerate the Adoption of Best Practices

4.1. Mandate Processes, Not Checklists, within Regulated Industries

The ability of the U.S. Government directly to impose cybersecurity standards across the millions (soon, billions) of domestic Internet-connected computers and devices is highly limited. Only a relatively tiny number of these devices are Government-owned or identifiably part of an industry that falls under existing Federal regulatory authorities. A perhaps larger, but still very small, fraction of these devices, while privately owned, may be identifiable as national critical infrastructure within the meaning of Executive Order 13636[11] and, as such, may be susceptible to some Federal regulation.

Finding: Many private-sector entities come under some form of Federal regulation for reasons not directly related to national security. In many such cases there is opportunity, fully consistent with the intent of the existing enabling legislation, for promoting and achieving best practices in cybersecurity.

We describe below just how this might work. PCAST's first caution, however, is that it is crucially important that such efforts not overstep their possible usefulness in any of three harmful ways:

- They must not be perceived as an effort to expand Federal regulatory reach to currently unregulated entities. For that reason, scope should be strictly limited to established boundaries of regulation, without advancement of novel legal theories proffered to stretch existing jurisdiction. Even a "voluntary" program for other industries, no matter how helpfully intended, may be perceived by industry as a problematic first step towards the assertion of new regulatory authorities.
- It would be an ineffective approach to create, within the Department of Homeland Security (DHS) or elsewhere, a centralized authoritative description of required cybersecurity measures. Such a list would rapidly become fossilized and bureaucratic, not just unproductive but counterproductive. Many examples of counterproductive mandated "check-off lists" exist.

- There needs to be a recognition that a one-size-fits-all approach will not work and that the focus needs to be on those elements that can have either impact at scale or cascading impact.

Recommendation: PCAST believes that, within already regulated industries, the preferred way to proceed is for the regulator to require not a specific list of cybersecurity measures but an auditable process by which cybersecurity best practices are adopted and continually improved.

For example, a regulated company should be required regularly to provide answers to these four questions:

1. How does the company determine what are the best practices for its industry?
2. What is the company's present state of conformity to those practices?
3. What is the company's plan and schedule for achieving full conformity?
4. How is the company ensuring that its best practices are improved and updated in response to evolving threats?

Since regulatory agencies will typically have the ability to comment, formally or informally, as to the adequacy of any company's specification, a constructive degree of encouragement could be adjusted on a company-by-company basis. Indeed, in tailoring the appropriate course and timing of actions with regard to a specific company or organization, careful consideration has to be given to the potential magnitude of consequences (including issues such as interdependency), or scaling effect, of a cyber security incident at an individual entity. NIST has an important convening role, on an ongoing basis, to assist with the development of an auditable process.

Publicly held companies that do not otherwise come under Federal regulation do come under regulatory authority of the Securities Exchange Commission (SEC), whose mission is to provide a level playing field for investors.[12] In that context, the SEC has the authority to mandate the disclosure of business risks by public companies under various circumstances (e.g., Form 10Q disclosures). By accounting practice, disclosed risks are "material." There is generally no necessity for a company to disclose risks whose consequences are small.

Cyber, however, is a new frontier. Because cyber risks can cascade, and are correlated across the whole economy, traditional standards of materiality may be naïve. For the purpose of providing investors with necessary risk information, the SEC might justifiably mandate that companies larger than a certain size, or in certain key sectors, should routinely disclose their cyber risk in a format that evaluates their responses against the appropriate industry best practice. The four numbered questions above can provide the appropriate logical structure. Indeed, at the end of 2011, SEC staff issued guidance that is relevant to this area, a small first step. However, stronger action is necessary at the Commission level for full and mandatory effect.[13]

We note that New York State's Department of Financial Services has sent formal requests that the state's large banks and three dozen large insurance companies disclose details on their preparedness for cyberattacks—requests that the recipients are legally obligated to answer.[14] This action is consistent with our view of what needs to be done with greater uniformity at the Federal level.

Recommendation: The President should strongly encourage independent regulatory agencies to adopt regulations that require self-reporting of continuous improvement practices along the lines discussed above. Particularly, the Securities and Exchange Commission should mandate, for publicly held companies, the disclosure, as investment risk factors, of the answers to the above four numbered questions.

4.2. Promote Creation of a Cyber-Safety Culture across Industry Broadly

The difference between the Federal Government's mandating specific, listed cyber practices—however such lists may be developed—versus its mandating auditable processes of continuous improvement, leaving the creation of best-practice specifics to the private sector, is worth further explication here. Either approach, at scale, will spawn the creation of a "compliance business," comprising specialized firms (or units within companies) that will advise on the details of technical compliance.

List-based mandates are likely to lead to a compliance business that will perceive incentives to minimal compliance. The commercially successful advisors will be those who are able to "check the boxes" for their clients at minimal cost, with the most success at negotiating with regulators, or litigating, the least onerous set of requirements. Check-off lists lead to a race to the compliance bottom. Specifically, PCAST urges DHS and NIST to exercise great caution in developing risk assessments or industry-specific compliance lists. PCAST is particularly doubtful that such assessments and lists can usefully keep up with the evolving threat.

By contrast, continuous-improvement mandates can motivate a race to the top, because expert third parties have incentive to become a part of the consensus process for what best practices should be. Such third parties would be likely to include cybersecurity researchers, management-consulting firms, and investment analysts in the private sector, and should also include leadership by Federal agencies such as NIST.[15] An industry that attempts to "get away with" practices inferior to those of another industry, and without a defensible industry-specific justification, will attract the attention of security professionals and others and produce pressure for improvement.

An analogous situation exists today in the human health and safety compliance business, where it has become accepted that the standard for companies in high-hazard activities should be founded on "safety culture," not just on checklists, and where there is an active industry of consulting and research that brings together the two threads of safety culture and continuous improvement. Each of these threads has a nuanced and well-studied history: continuous improvement originating in the post-World War II work of statisticians W. Edwards Deming and Joseph M. Juran (who are credited with spurring Japan's kaizen [continuous improvement] revolution in the 1950s), and safety culture exemplified by such American companies as DuPont.[16] Federal policy should be designed to provide incentives for the analogous continually improving cybersecurity safety culture, rather than minimal compliance with a mandated, and likely soon-out-of-date, list.

Finding: Industry-driven, but third-party audited, continuous improvement processes are more likely to create an effective cybersecurity culture than are Government-mandated, static lists of security measures.

Recommendation: For the private sector, Government's role should be to encourage continuously improving, consensus-based standards and transparent reporting of whether those standards are being met by individual private-sector entities.

We note the U.S. General Services Administration's FedRAMP program as one effort at defining best practices (in this case, for cloud computing products and services) and using accrediting third-party assessors for auditing conformity to such practices.[17] More recently, in response to Executive Order 13636 and Presidential Policy Directive 21, NIST has initiated a cybersecurity framework process that appears fully consistent with the intent of PCAST's finding.[18]

V. DYNAMIC, REAL-TIME RESPONSE HAS BECOME ESSENTIAL

The cybersecurity threat has changed dramatically, a shift that has been noted not just within the U.S. Government, but also by the private sector and internationally. While China's highly publicized intrusions have garnered the most attention,[19] the change has been recognized earlier and more broadly.[20] It is now apparent that ongoing, concerted efforts at good hygienic and operational practices, even coupled to improved hardening by the software developers and advanced intrusion detection and antimalware systems, will not be sufficient to protect computer systems from advanced forms of cyber-attacks.

Specifically, some forms of cyber-attack are designed to propagate at very high rates, and the non-real-time nature of the various forms of hardening, updates, and delivery of signatures means that these approaches do not provide for the rapid and widespread reaction needed to prevent serious damage. This shortcoming has been compounded by the rapid diversification of the types of devices that are attached to the Internet, including phones, tablets, automobiles, and a wide variety of consumer appliances. Most of these devices have not been designed with sophisticated hardening or other types of defense mechanisms. This leaves them particularly vulnerable to dynamic alteration of the applications running on them. These vulnerabilities become all the more worrisome in light of the trend, in the kinds of attacks being mounted, toward destructive malware as opposed to network-based denial-of-service attacks.

The biggest practical challenges lie in predicting or recognizing the attack and determining how to mitigate it in real-time. In this connection, the fact that so much of cyberspace is in the hands of the private sector motivates interest in finding ways to interconnect its monitoring, surveillance, and forensic capabilities with those of the Government. Doing so would be challenging technically, however, as well as subject to legal and policy constraints that currently exist both within the United States and internationally.

For example, the Electronic Communications Privacy Act of 1986 (ECPA, 18 USC 2702) prohibits private sector entities providing electronic communication services from disclosing customer information (such as identity) to the Government, even when the entity observes illegal activity by the customer, and even when it is in the broader interest of its other customers that law enforcement be informed. ECPA provides only a small number of designated exceptions to this general prohibition (see below). Today, customers include virtually all users of the Internet, and communication services encompass virtually all uses of the Internet. Although the so-called business-records provision of the USA PATRIOT Act (50 USC 1861) may have authorized the release of some customer data to Government, it seems likely to remain the case that use of data available to the private sector will be primarily by the private sector itself. Rather than attempting to prognosticate the likelihood, or even direction, of future legislative changes, PCAST restricts its proposed recommendations to those that seem feasible now.

Finding: To improve the capacity to respond in real time, cyberthreat data need to be shared more extensively among private-sector entities and—in appropriate circumstances and with publicly understood interfaces—between private-sector entities and Government.

By its original intent, ECPA does not regulate communications purely among private-sector entities; it applies only to communications with the Government, and it explicitly exempts disclosures "to any person other than a Governmental entity." Moreover, it is among private-sector entities that the exchange of threat information is now most badly needed. Some nascent private-sector organizations are attempting to fill this need.[21]

Recommendations

- The Federal Government should act to facilitate the establishment of private-sector partnerships for the real-time exchange of threat data among potentially vulnerable private-sector entities. Data flows among these privatesector entities should not and would not be accessible by the Government. The Federal Government might participate in establishing protocols, or providing technology, for how the data are utilized by the private sector for its own cyberdefense. The protocols or technology utilized should have sufficient transparency to mitigate legitimate concerns about inappropriate Government access to private data.

Finding: Internet Service Providers are well-positioned to contribute to rapid improvements in cybersecurity through real-time action.

Internet Service Providers (ISPs) are well-positioned, both technically and by their relationship with their customers, to contribute to rapid improvements in cybersecurity that exploit dynamic, real-time response possibilities.[22] The ISPs control the actual connection of their customers to the Internet—the so-called first hop. As just one example, ISPs are uniquely able to do ingress validation, checking that the connected machine is identifying itself honestly. In some situations, ISPs have both the means to detect compromised machines quickly (for example, machines recruited into a botnet) and the ability to do something about them—for example, to notify the customer and provide options for fixing the problem. Lacking both a legal obligation to act and any protection against subsequent liability, however, such action by ISPs is quite rare. This needs to be changed.

Recommendations

- The Federal Government should establish policies that describe the desired behavior by ISPs as best (or minimum-acceptable) practices.
- The National Institute of Standards and Technology (NIST) should work with ISPs towards establishing standards for voluntary measures by which ISPs can alert users and direct them to appropriate resources when their machines or devices are known to be compromised.

It would not make sense to take actions that break the business model of ISPs, for example by requiring large new investments in expensive customer service or by creating ill-will with customers. But ISPs could offer, as a competitive or revenue opportunity, additional services that could be provided immediately, even on compromised machines—for example, controlled web browsing and access to email. Many customers might pay another dollar or two monthly for the guarantee of such services, a kind of cybersecurity insurance policy. Analogous products for compromised cell phones and other devices could also be provided.

VI. New Engineering Methodologies and New Software Architectures Are Needed

In the long run, if cyberthreats are to be countered effectively, the Nation's approach to systems architectures must be rethought.

Finding: Future architectures will need to start with the premise that each part of a system must be designed to operate in a hostile environment. Research is needed to foster systems with dynamic, real-time defenses to complement hardening approaches.

These principles apply to all levels of the "technology stack" (i.e., the layers of components or services that make up the connected system in question), and must include the hardware itself, plus the firmware and software layers that are built on top.

Recommendations

- The Nation's research universities and industry laboratories should be more directly partnered in the creation of high-assurance computing systems, including hardware, firmware, and the complete software stack.
- An organization should be tasked with the development of certifiable maturity levels with respect to threat-aware design processes for companies that design hardware and software. The Software Engineering Institute (SEI), a Federally Funded Research and Development Center with a Department of Defense (DoD) charter, could be so tasked by DoD. A separate hardware or networking--related activity may also be needed, perhaps at MITRE Corporation's National Security Engineering Center, which also has a DoD charter. Microsoft's publicly available Security Development Lifecycle (SDL) is achieving significant adoption in the private sector and could be a starting point. The certification of maturity levels has proved to be an effective means for driving best engineering practices, and it should be harnessed in service of cybersecurity.
- In addition to these intermediate-term cybersecurity R&D activities, the Nation should invest in high-risk, high-return basic research with a

10to20year time horizon that, if successful, could fundamentally transform the future cybersecurity landscape.

End Notes

[1] The acronyms are "commercial off-the-shelf" and "government off-the-shelf," respectively.

[2] Center for Strategic and International Studies. "The Economic Impact of Cybercrime and Cyber Espionage." July 2013 http://www.mcafee.com/us/resources/reports/rp-economic-impact-cybercrime.pdf.

[3] Botnets are sets, sometimes numbering as many as millions, of private computers infected with malicious software and controlled as a group without their owners' knowledge.

[4] For example, in November 2010, the arrest in Russia of a single individual caused global email spam to drop (temporarily) by 20%. See: Kramer, Andrew E. "Email Spam Falls After Russian Crackdown."The New York Times. Web. 26 Oct. 2010 http://www.nytimes.com/2010/10/27/business/27spam.html.

[5] See link associated with the National Strategy for Trusted Identities in Cyberspace in: Daniel, Michael. "Collaborative and Cross-Cutting Approaches to Cybersecurity."The White House Blog. Web. 01 Aug. 2012 http://www.whitehouse.gov/blog/2012/08/01/collaborative-and-cross-cutting-approaches-cybersecurity.

[6] The three priorities are trusted Internet connections, continuous monitoring of Federal information systems, and strong (non-password) authentication. An updated White House blog posting is: Daniel, Michael. "Cross Agency Priority Goal: Cybersecurity." Web. 2013 http://goals.performance.gov/content/cybersecurity.

[7] See link associated with the Electric Sector Capability Maturity Model in: Daniel, Michael. "Collaborative and Cross-Cutting Approaches to Cybersecurity." The White House Blog. Web. 01 Aug. 2012 http://www.whitehouse.gov/blog/2012/08/01/collaborative-and-cross-cutting-approaches-cybersecurity.

[8] See link associated with End-User Cybersecurity Protection in: Daniel, Michael. "Collaborative and Cross-Cutting Approaches to Cybersecurity." The White House Blog. Web. 01 Aug. 2012 http://www.whitehouse.gov/blog/2012/08/01/collaborative-and-cross-cutting-approaches-cybersecurity.

[9] Executive Order 13636. "Improving Critical Infrastructure Cybersecurity" Federal Register. vol. 78, no. 33, p. 11739. 12 Feb. 2013 http://www.whitehouse.gov/the-press-office/2013/02/12/executive-order-improving-critical-infrastructure-cybersecurity.

[10] Presidential Policy Directive (PPD21). "Critical Infrastructure Security and Resilience." Web. 12 Feb. 2013 http://www.whitehouse.gov/the-pressoffice/2013/02/12/presidential-policy-directive-critical-infrastructure-security-and-resil.

[11] The referenced Executive Order defines critical infrastructure as those "systems and assets, whether physical or virtual, so vital to the United States that the incapacity or destruction of such systems and assets would have a debilitating impact on security, national economic security, national public health or safety, or any combination of those matters."

[12] The consumer protection mission of the Federal Trade Commission, focused on countering deception and/or unfair business practices, provides another broad umbrella that has been used to encourage companies to do more to strengthen cybersecurity.

[13] See, for example: Strohm, Chris. "SEC Chairman Reviewing Company Cybersecurity Disclosures." Bloomberg. Web. 13 May 2013 http://www.bloomberg.com/news/2013-05-13/sec-chairman-reviewing-company-cybersecurity-disclosures.html. For a different point of view, see: Mutch, John. "Beware The Coming SEC Regulations On Cybersecurity." Forbes. Web. 15 May 2013 http://www.forbes.com/sites/ ciocentral/ 2013/05/15/how-to-prepare-for-when-the-sec-comes-asking-about-cybersecurity-risk/.

[14] Berkowitz, Ben. "NY Regulator Asks Insurers about Readiness for Cyber Threats." Reuters. Web. 28 May 2013 http://www.reuters.com/article/2013/05/28/usa-cybersecurity-insurance-newyork-idUSL2N0E919B20130528.

[15] An additional source of third-party expertise is the set of security-configuration guidelines for the prevalent ecosystem products that are published by the Information Assurance Directorate of the National Security Agency. The Federal Government should adopt these guidelines immediately for its own systems. See: The National Security Agency. "Security Configuration Guidelines." Web. 16 Sept. 2013 http://cee.che.ufl.edu/AIChE_CEE_Klein_DuPont_Extended.pdf.

[16] Klein, James A. "Two Centuries of Process Safety at DuPont." Process Safety Progress. vol. 28, no. 2, pp. 113122. June 2009 http://cee.che.ufl.edu/AIChE_CEE_ Klein_DuPont_Extended.pdf.

[17] Federal Risk and Authorization Management Program (FedRAMP). http://www.gsa.gov/portal/ category/102371?utm_source=OCSIT&utm_term=fedramp.

[18] 18. "NIST Releases Preliminary Cybersecurity Framework, Will Seek Comments." Press release, October 22, 2013. http://www.nist.gov/itl/cybersecurity102213.cfm.

[19] Examples include: Perlroth, Nicole. "Hackers in China Attacked The Times for Last 4 Months."The New York Times. Web. 30 Jan. 2013 http://www.nytimes.com/2013/01/31/technology/chinese-hackers-in-filtrate-newyork-times- computers.html?pagewanted=all&_r=0; Perlroth, Nicole. "Wall Street Journal Announces That It, Too, Was Hacked by the Chinese." The New York Times. Web. 31 Jan. 2013 http://www.nytimes.com/2013/01/31/technology/chinese-hackers-infiltrate-newyork-timescomputers.html?pagewanted=all&_r=0; Perlroth, Nicole. "Washington Post Joins List of News Media Hacked by the Chinese." The New York Times. Web. 1 Feb. 2013 http://www.nytimes.com/2013/02/02/technology/washington-posts-joins-list-of-media-hacked-by-the-chinese.html; Sanger, David E., David Barboza, and Nicole Perlroth. "Chinese Army Unit Is Seen as Tied to Hacking Against U.S." The New York Times. Web. 18 Feb. 2013 http://www.nytimes.com/2013/02/19/technology/chinas-army-is-seen-as-tied-to-hacking-against-us.html?pagewanted=all; and Mandiant Corporation. "APT1: Exposing One of China's Cyber Espionage Units." 2013. http://intelreport.mandiant.com/.

[20] Examples include: For example: Gjelten, Tom. "Cybersecurity Firms Ditch Defense, Learn to 'Hunt." NPR Morning Edition. Web. 10 May 2012 http://www.npr.org/2012/05/10/152374358/cybersecurity-firms-ditch-defense-learn-to-hunt; Nakashima, Ellen. "Cybersecurity should be more active, official says." The Washington Post. Web. 16 Sept. 2012 http://articles.washingtonpost.com/20120916/world/35494752_1_top-cyber-private-sector-crowdstrike; Perlroth, Nicole. "Outmaneuvered at Their Own Game, Antivirus Makers Struggle to Adapt."The New York Times. Web. 31 Dec. 2012 http://www.nytimes.com/2013/01/01/technology/antivirus-makers-work-on-software-to-catch-malware-more-effectively.html?pagewanted=all.

[21] Martinez, Jennifer. "Former DHS deputy secretary launches cybersecurity council." The Hill. Web. 14 Aug. 2012 http://thehill.com/blogs/hillicon-valley/technology/316611former-dhs-deputy-secretary-launches-cybersecurity-council.

[22] Where customers have more than one choice of ISP, they are able to choose the one that offers, in their view, the greatest value or trust. This makes the relationship to some degree voluntary rather than imposed.

INDEX

D

E

F

G

H

I

J

L

M

N

O

S

T

U

V

W